STAYING MARRIED IN A DEGENERATE AGE

By

MICHAEL SEBASTIAN

STAYING MARRIED IN A DEGENERATE AGE

Copyright © 2016 by Michael Sebastian

TABLE OF CONTENTS

Introduction

There is a war going on. The goal of the war is to fundamentally transform human society. There are many fronts in this war, but the brunt of the attack is targeted at the institution that serves as the foundation for society—traditional marriage.

Never in the history of humanity has society been more unfavorable to traditional marriage. Divorce, which was once vilified, is now portrayed as an empowering and liberating experience. Approximately 40% of marriages end in divorce.

The rate of marital infidelity is high: about 23% of men and 19% of women cheat on their spouses—and some studies estimate that the rates are much higher for both sexes.

Young people are abandoning marriage in droves. It is estimated that 25% of millennials will never marry—that is the highest rate of unmarried people in modern times.

There are also troubling movements of people that believe that marriage, as an institution is so flawed that they have abandoned it all together. One such group is the "Men Going Their Own Way" (MGTOW) movement. These men are so afraid of marrying in the prevailing conditions that they have given up hope that they will ever marry. Some of these men will have sex with women, but they will never commit. Others foreswear women entirely as not being worth the effort.

The percentage of out-of-wedlock births continues to rise. In 1980, 18.4% of births were out-of-wedlock but by 2010 the figure rose to 40.8%. For women under age 30, *at least half of births are now out-of-wedlock*. As bad as that is, the number for some communities is even more staggering. The rate of out-of-wedlock births in the African-American community is 72%!

But all of this is not the worst part. There are groups of people who have made it their mission to destroy traditional marriage. These people have a utopian vision for society and they view marriage as an impediment to achieving that vision. These groups are well funded and politically connected, and they won't be happy until they are victorious.

But this book is not about these negative forces that are attacking marriage. This book is for men and women who want to fight to save marriage and who believe the best way of doing that is by building strong marriages.

This book will provide you with concrete, practical ideas to:

- Cheat-proof your marriage.
- Use effective communication skills.
- Inject romance back into your marriage.
- Eliminate boredom.
- Avoid the money traps that ensnare many couples.
- Understand the media messages that attack traditional marriage.
- Protect your marriage against negative cultural influences.
- Strengthen your faith to keep your marriage solid.
- Implement a realistic spiritual program for yourself and your family.
- Help husbands become more "alpha male" and assume a leadership role for their families.

If you are still single and looking to get married, this book will serve as an excellent marriage preparation manual. I've included a chapter on what qualities to look for in a future spouse. There's also a chapter dedicated to what men and women want in a wife or husband—information that can give you an advantage in the dating market.

1. A Perfect Marriage

While I was in college, I attended a midwestern mega church. The church service frequently included a layman and his wife giving a short talk about their lives. The couples were invariably young and attractive, which made sense given that the church attracted a lot of college students. It gave students a goal to shoot for. Who wouldn't want to be married to a handsome Christian man or beautiful Christian woman?

The talks took two basic forms. Either the husband was leading a dissolute life as a playboy until he became a Christian, at which point he met his gorgeous wife and then everything fell into place, or the couple was experiencing marital problems until they became Christian and they lived happily ever after. In other words, their marriages were perfect.

I am here to say that there is no such thing as perfect marriage. Building a successful marriage takes work and there is never a point where you can just take your spouse or your marriage for granted. Furthermore, there is no silver bullet that will make your marriage 100% divorce proof, especially in our current divorce-happy culture. And sadly, becoming a Christian is no guarantee of a fairy tale life—one glance at the divorce statistics for Christians will confirm this truth.

I don't think the mega church that I attended was being disingenuous. The testimony of those young couples was generally true, but I am sure they were leaving their struggles out of their talks. After all, few people want to stand up in front of a large group of their peers and talk about their problems.

However, while the talks were well intentioned, I believe they were ultimately damaging because they set an unrealistic standard for marriage. If a couple is conditioned to think that marriage is a bed of roses, sans the thorns, they will inevitably be disappointed once they find themselves in the midst of troubles.

My Own Marriage

While my wife and I have a good marriage, I can't say that it is perfect. We are both Catholic Christians so we came into our marriage with the full intention of making it "till death do us part," but good intentions are not enough to make a marriage survive. The first year of our marriage was extraordinarily difficult. Neither one of us committed some egregious fault, it is just that we were both bad communicators—and I was failing in my duties as a husband to lead.

It started during the wedding planning. My wife received little guidance or assistance from her family so all the work of coordinating fell to her. She looked to me to help, but she didn't ask me for it and I wasn't paying enough attention to notice. So our marriage started off with some resentment.

Instead of overcoming the resentment, I exacerbated it. My wife had to wake up very early because of her long commute to work. Any emotionally mature person would have taken this in stride, but I resented the new schedule. I would wake up grouchy every morning. This lead to fights over petty things. Before long, it was looking like our marriage was going to hit the rocks before it had even set sail.

It wasn't that we were not communicating. We spent abundant time together and we talked a lot, but our communication was about things that didn't really matter. We talked about work, world events, politics, and celebrities, but not about the issues in our marriage. The only time we did actually communicate was during arguments—and that was the time when we were both the least receptive to listening.

Being a man, my natural inclination was to go in and "fix the problem," but when I asked my wife exactly what was wrong, she wasn't able to fully put her feelings into words. I found that I was having the same difficulty in verbalizing exactly what I was feeling.

How did we turn it around? I realized that we were locked in a vicious cycle: my grouchiness fed her anger, which, in turn, made me more resentful. The first step, therefore, was to break the cycle. Instead of being grouchy, I decided to wake up happy. I adopted a cheerful disposition, which I have held to unswervingly.

The results were not immediate, and I did not expect them to be. In his book, *Seven Habits of Highly Effective People*, Stephen R. Covey writes about the concept of an "emotional bank account." Every time a person does something bad to you, they make a withdrawal from the emotional bank account. Every time a person does something good for you, they make a deposit to the emotional bank account. I knew that my behavior had put me into the red with my wife's emotional bank account. It would take many "deposits" to put me back in the black.

But eventually, we did get back—and then some. We have been married for 11 years and our marriage is flourishing. That doesn't mean it is perfect, and it doesn't mean that we can rest on our laurels. Marriage will always take work, but it is joyful work, not drudgery.

I am convinced that if you put the principles of this book into practice, your marriage will not just survive, but thrive.

An Objection

By the way, you may be thinking: "Why was it your duty to change? Why didn't your wife have to change as well?"

It's a good question. I also happen to be a weekly columnist at the website called *Return of Kings*, which is aimed at men. The writers and commenters on *Return of Kings* are very critical of men who put undeserving women on a pedestal and take all the blame when something goes wrong.

I want to be very clear that I am not advocating that men take all the blame. They can only assume the blame for their own behavior, not the behavior of their wife. In my case, the lion's share of the blame was on me because I was not acting as the leader of my family. Rather than setting the pace, I was acting irrationally. My wife was merely reflecting the energy that I was emitting.

Once I corrected my behavior, it was up to my wife to change her behavior in response to my changes. Marriage is never a one-way street. Both partners are responsible and need to give 100%.

Despite this, men do have a special role. Men must be the spiritual leaders of their family. A true leader always has the most responsibility and the biggest burden. I will discuss the concept of spiritual leadership in much greater detail in a later chapter.

Before we dive into the ways to stay married, the first thing to do is to understand where marriage came from.

2. Where Did Marriage Come From?

Most people never give any thought to the institutions of society. They simply assume that everything is arbitrary and, therefore, infinitely malleable. One of the institutions that lots of Americans believe is arbitrary is marriage. Even Christians, who purport to believe that marriage is something more than just a chance arrangement, often act and vote in ways that would lead one to question their sincerity.

The fact that Americans feel that marriage is an arbitrary institution can be seen by the recent introduction of same sex-marriage. Even if the Supreme Court had not imposed it by judicial fiat, same-sex marriage gradually would have been implemented democratically on a state-by-state basis. Same-sex marriage was steadily gaining in popularity—the most recent Wall Street Journal poll numbers showed that 59% percent of Americans supported same sex marriage—and there was no sign of the trend reversing.

But is marriage really a completely arbitrary institution that is imposed on us by our culture? Did it only come about because of the rise of Christianity? To understand the roots of our current confusion, we have to go back to the 19th century.

The "Marriage is a Social Construct" Myth

There is a popular myth that marriage is a cultural construct that only became popular with the rise of Christianity. The purveyors of this myth believe that prehistoric man behaved like an animal—men would have sex with whatever woman they could get their hands on. The purveyors of this myth also believe that before the ancient Romans adopted Christianity, a "free love" situation existed among the pagans. The idea is that Christian marriage is an artificial imposition upon man's naturally promiscuous nature.

This myth has its basis in evolutionary theory. In the wake of the publication of Charles Darwin's *Origin of the Species* in 1859, anthropologists of the late 19th century reasoned that if humans evolved from animals, it is only logical that early man's social behavior was very close to that of animals.

The Influence of Margaret Mead

The idea that marriage is a cultural construct got a big boost with the writings of anthropologist Margaret Mead. Mead theorized that westerners were sexually repressed due to the influence of Christianity. To find out how humans really behaved in their "natural" state, Mead would have to find a group of people who had been, in her eyes, untainted by Christian morality.

Mead chose to study the inhabitants of the Samoan islands because the Samoans were in the early stages of converting to Christianity, and many of their tribal customs and morality were still in place. Mead spent most of her time studying adolescent girls, apparently because she thought this group would be the best source of information on Samoan sexual practices.

Coming of Age in Samoa

Mead documented the results of her study in the 1928 book entitled *Coming of Age in Samoa*. She wrote that Samoans did not experience the same level of sexual neuroses as westerners. According to Mead, Samoans were very relaxed about extramarital sexual relations. Premarital sex was supposedly common and it was not necessarily considered wrong.

The book was a bombshell that sent shockwaves through the academic community. Here at last was "proof" that humans were naturally promiscuous just as evolutionary theory had predicted. Her theory of the relaxed and simple natural state of man was eagerly taken up by the elites of the day who wanted to liberate themselves from Christian morality. It became the orthodoxy of the day. Generations of college students were indoctrinated into

Mead's theories were a huge influence on the sexual liberation movement of the 1960s.

Mead's Conclusions Challenged

Belief in Mead's work was so entrenched in academia that when another anthropologist tried to publish a work challenging her conclusions back in 1971, he was rejected. That anthropologist, Derek Freeman, finally did publish the book in 1983. In his book *Margaret Mead in Samoa: the Making and Unmaking of an Anthropological Myth*, Freeman debunked every major conclusion that Mead had made. For example, far from being unconcerned with a bride's virginity, Samoans were so concerned that they had a ritual to ensure that women were virgins on their wedding day. The ritual, which is shocking by our standards, is that the husband would pierce his bride's hymen *in public* so that she would be unable to deceive her husband. Samoa was hardly the relaxed, sexually permissive society that Mead had reported.

Why was Mead so far off base? In short, it was because Mead had come to Samoa with preconceived ideas. She believed that she would find that the Samoans were closer to primitive promiscuity; the state that she thought humans originally existed in. She saw in Samoan society what she had expected to see.

Old Myths Die Hard

Despite the fact that her research has been debunked, Margaret Mead's theories live on in the public consciousness even if the vast majority of people have never heard of her. The idea of "free love" jibes with what people envision the life of a cave man (another figment of the popular imagination) to have been. The idea of primitive promiscuity also supports the very appealing idea that we have a basis for casting off Christian morality and living our lives as we please.

Evolutionary psychology has also been used to support the idea that marriage is an arbitrary institution and that primitive promiscuity prevailed in early humans. Evolutionary psychology tries to determine how humans should behave by looking at the behavior of lower animals, especially primates. One of the favorites of evolutionary psychologists is the bonobo or pygmy chimpanzee.

Bonobos

Bonobos have what might be called a matriarchal society. The female bonobos continue to collect food (fruit, nuts, and insects) even as they are caring for their offspring so the males are not needed to protect the females. Thus bonobos do not form permanent monogamous sexual relationships.

That is not so very surprising as only about 3% of animals form monogamous relationships, but evolutionary psychologists are interested in them for other reasons as well. Bonobos are quite promiscuous. Both male and female bonobos trade sex for food, and sex is used to diffuse tension in the bonobo group. They are one of the few primates that engage in oral sex as well as homosexual sex. And, last but not least, in bonobo societies, the females are more dominant than the males.

Evolutionary psychologists would hold up bonobo society as a model for our own. It is everything they would like our society to be: female dominated, promiscuous, sometimes homosexual, and peaceful.

But Are Humans Really Like Bonobos?

Learning about bonobos can be fascinating, but the fact that evolutionary psychologists have chosen bonobos to be the norm for humans tells us more about those psychologists than it does about humans. This seems to be another case of the Margaret Mead syndrome where researchers see what they expect to see.

Why? Because researchers could just as easily hold chimpanzees as the model for humans, but that would lead to some uncomfortable conclusions. You see, chimpanzees, unlike bonobos, are a male-dominated society. While bonobos have a very informal pecking order, chimpanzees are a very strict hierarchy with an alpha male atop the pyramid. And unlike the irenic bonobos, chimpanzees are aggressive.

But our cultural elite disfavors concepts like aggression, hierarchy, and being patriarchal, so bonobos are preferred over the chimpanzee model. So at the end of the day, observing these animals does not tell us very much about what humans *should* act like after all.

Marriage in History

Not all evolutionary psychologists agree that ancient humans were promiscuous like lower primates. They reason that early man did possess an institution similar to marriage because of the nature of human infants. Human babies are helpless for much longer than any other animal. During the time that a mother is caring for her child, she needs extra protection. Thus, theorists speculate that when a father stayed around to protect the mother and child, his offspring would have an advantage over the offspring of fathers who left the mother.

While this paternal care theory makes sense, it remains, like all insights of evolutionary psychology, in the realm of pure speculation. If we really want to know how marriage was practiced in the past, we have to look to history.

There is a common misconception—fueled by the "marriage is a social construct" myth—that monogamous marriage is Christian in origin. Modern society, through academia and popular culture, teaches that lifelong fidelity in marriage is unnatural, and the only reason it came into being is because of the teaching of Christ.

14

But if monogamous marriage were the result of the acceptance of Christianity, then we would expect that the pagan civilizations that preceded it did not have monogamous marriage. Perhaps the pagans, unsaddled with the oppressive baggage of Christian dogma, were free to love whoever and however they pleased.

Unfortunately for the modern critics, the Greek and Roman civilizations did practice monogamous marriage—and they were a lot stricter about it than we are today.

For example, in our modern society, a divorce is relatively easy to obtain. A couple no longer even needs a reason to file for a divorce. Couples can practice what actress Gwyneth Paltrow called "conscious uncoupling."

Marriage in the Ancient World

But in the ancient world, a divorce was very difficult to obtain. French historian Numa Denis Fustel de Coulanges explains in *The Ancient City*:

> Marriage was indissoluble, and divorce was almost impossible. The Roman law did indeed permit the dissolution of the marriage... but the dissolution of the religious marriage was very difficult. For that, a new sacred ceremony was necessary, as religion alone could separate what religion had united.

"Free love" was also unknown among the barbarian tribes that eventually conquered the Roman Empire. The Roman historian Tacitus writes of the Germanic tribes that:

> The marriage bond is strict, and no feature in their mode of life is more creditable to them than this... They are content with one wife: very few of them have more than one, and these few exceptions are not due to wantonness; they are cases of men of high rank, to whom several matrimonial alliances have been offered from motives of policy.

Regarding the sexual morality of the barbarians, Tacitus goes on to say:

> They guard the chastity of their lives with no shows to entice them, nor orgies to excite their evil passions. To men and women alike such a thing as secret correspondence is unknown. Amongst all this immense population adultery is extremely rare.

Thus, these ancient cultures give no support to the proposition that it was Christianity that came in and spoiled all the fun. As C.S. Lewis writes: "Men have differed as to whether you should have one wife or four. But they have always agreed that you must not simply have any woman you liked."

Christian Marriage

While Christianity is not responsible for creating marriage, it did up the ante by declaring that marriage is indissoluble. Once you contract a valid marriage, you are married for the rest of your life. Not even adultery can break the marriage bond. The Romans and the Germans, as strict as they were, were not that strict.

The Jewish doctrine of divorce is found in the teaching of Moses:

> When a man has taken a wife, and married her, and it come to pass that she find no favor in his eyes, because he has found *some uncleanness in her*: then let him write her a bill of divorce, and give it in her hand, and send her out of his house. (Deuteronomy 24:1)

Within first century Judaism there were two schools of interpretation for what Moses meant by the word "uncleanness." The school of Hillel gave the word a very liberal interpretation saying that it meant that a husband could put away his wife *for any cause*, even burning a meal.

The school of Shammai, on the other hand, took a more conservative approach. They interpreted Deuteronomy 24:1 to mean that a husband could only divorce his wife for something extremely shameful, like adultery.

In other words, these schools of interpretation did not question the *legitimacy* of divorce; only what *reasons* would be acceptable to obtain a divorce. Understanding these two schools of Jewish interpretation is critical as background to comprehending the teaching of Jesus on marriage.

The most complete statement of Jesus on marriage is found in Matthew 19. The context of the passage is that some Pharisees approach Jesus to test him. They ask, "Is it lawful for a man to divorce his wife for any cause?" (Matthew 19:3).

The question is a trap. If Jesus says that divorce is not lawful, the Pharisees will accuse him of blasphemy for putting himself above Scripture. But if Jesus permitted divorce, they could say that his teaching fell short of the perfection that was expected of the Messiah.

Jesus ignores the false dichotomy that the Pharisees have laid before him. Rather, he points his hearers back to the very foundation of marriage in Genesis:

> Have you not read that the one who made them at the beginning 'made them male and female,' and said, 'For this reason a man shall leave his father and mother and be joined to his wife, and the two shall become one flesh'? So they are no longer two, but one flesh. Therefore what God has joined together, let no one separate. (Matthew 19:4-6).

The Pharisees immediately understand that what Jesus just said is stricter than either contemporary rabbinic teaching or Mosaic Law. So they respond asking, "Why then did Moses command us to give a certificate of dismissal and to divorce her?" (Matthew 19:7).

Jesus responds by pointing out that Mosaic Law's teaching on this point was a concession: "It was because you were so hard-hearted that Moses allowed you to divorce your wives, but from the beginning it was not so." (Matthew 19:8). Then Jesus, using his own authority, provides the original intention of marriage:

> And I say to you, whoever divorces his wife, except for sexual immorality, and marries another commits adultery. (Matthew 19:9).

This response is so shocking that it causes Jesus' disciples to say, "If such is the case of a man with his wife, it is better not to marry."

There is a debate among biblical scholars as to the meaning of the clause, *except for sexual immorality*. The phrase *sexual immorality* is a translation of the Greek word *porneia*. There have been gallons of ink spilled over what the word means in the context of this passage. Some scholars take *porneia* to mean any sex outside of the marriage, so they would interpret Jesus' words as meaning that the only acceptable reason to divorce is adultery. Other scholars interpret *porneia* more narrowly, suggesting that it may refer Jewish consanguinity laws.

While the debate may be interesting, there is a better way of determining the meaning directly from the passage itself. If Jesus had meant to allow divorce in cases where a spouse commits adultery, he would have been saying the same thing as the school of Shammai—something that would have been considered uncontroversial to all of his listeners. The fact that the disciples are shocked suggests that Jesus was taking a much harder line than even Shammai—Jesus was saying that marriage could not be dissolved even if one of the parties committed adultery.

If this is the correct interpretation, we find it just a shocking today as Jesus' listeners did 2000 years ago.

Regardless of whether you agree with the above exegesis, I believe the one thing that all Christians can agree on is that divorce needs to be very, very rare. It's a great scandal that the rates of divorce for Christians are at about the same level as those for the general population.

Tying It All Together

Our culture wants us to believe that marriage is a social construct that was created relatively recently in the history of humanity. History tells a different story. Marriage has been with us from very beginning. And monogamous marriage is not some invention of Christianity. On the contrary, many pagan civilizations had a higher view of marriage than our own.

Today, however, the institution of marriage is under a withering attack. The next chapter covers the origins of the attack.

3. The War on the Marriage

The traditional family of husband, wife, and children is under attack in the modern world. It is crucial for all married people to understand the nature of this attack and its sources.

Some of the attack is inadvertent—our society simply is not organized to encourage or support marriage. Rather, our system of isolated nuclear families with little extended family support makes it difficult on marriages.

However, other parts of the attack are deliberate attempts by various groups to either redefine or even completely eliminate the institution of marriage. We cannot afford to be ignorant of their agenda.

I'll discuss the inadvertent attack from consumerism and corporations; then I will cover how groups are using the government to undermine traditional marriage.

Consumerism

President Coolidge famously said, "The business of America is business." While that quote might be a bit of hyperbole, it is not far from the truth. Our capitalistic system has provided Americans with untold wealth versus the rest of the world, and while there are some signs that American capitalism is beginning to struggle under the weight of excessive regulation, it is still one of the best places to start a business.

But there is also a dark side to capitalism. The first is consumerism. Companies like Apple have specialized in creating needs for things that never existed before. But these new "necessities" usually turn out to be expensive and they only have a shelf life of about a year before the hot new version comes out. It is easy to get caught on the hamster wheel of "success" where one works long hours to buy more stuff. But buying more things requires even more work that takes spouses away from each other and their children.

Consumerism is not so much a deliberate attack on marriage as it is a threat. If couples let themselves or their children get sucked into it, it takes our focus off what is important (health and family) and puts it on what is unimportant (getting more stuff).

Corporations

Another inadvertent attack on the traditional family comes from corporations. Corporations are not bad in and of themselves— they exist to turn a profit for their stockholders. In theory, corporations should be agnostic when it comes to marriage and the family. In practice, corporations have been on the cutting edge in the effort to redefine marriage.

Corporations have been quick to provide benefits to same-sex couples, well before same-sex marriage became the law of the land. Additionally, corporations have been big supporters of LGBTQ issues by funding and supporting political candidates who are working to implement an agenda that is favorable to the LGBTQ cause.

Corporations are also supporters of women in the workplace. While corporations want to appear to be "pro-woman" on the surface, their real goal is to encourage women, including mothers, to dedicate more time to work and less time to their families.

In 1960, women made up about 33% of the workforce. Today, women comprise half of all workers. The increase is due of the large number of mothers that have entered the workforce after the sexual revolution of the 1960s.

But why would corporations want more mothers to work? Increasing the percentage of women in the workplace makes sense from a sheer economic perspective. If companies can increase the supply of workers, the price that they will have to pay each worker goes down. It is simply the law of supply and demand.

The support of LGBTQ related issues is similarly driven by the bottom line. It is estimated that only 2% of the population is gay or lesbian. Of that 2%, only a subset of people will ever want to contract a same-sex marriage. On first glance, it seems like a small market.

However, it is not only the LGBTQ market that companies are after. Companies want to be seen as forward thinking. If they see the culture shifting in one direction, they are quick to jump on the trend and tout it in their public relations. An example of this is all the companies that were producing commercials with same-sex couples long before same-sex marriage became the law of the land. This corporate support accelerated the acceptance of alternative lifestyles.

We can expect that as society continues to undermine traditional marriage, corporations will continue to be on the forefront of accepting and encouraging those changes.

The State

All throughout history, there has been a tension between the state and the family. The first goal of the state is to ensure that its citizens are loyal to it. Therefore, anything that can infringe on that loyalty is viewed with suspicion.

There are some obvious things—such as loyalty to a foreign power—that can come between a state and the individual. But there are also some less obvious things such as religious belief and the family.

Rome

You can see this in the ancient Roman practice of emperor worship. Rome was a very diverse empire—it had conquered many different ethnic groups with differing languages and religions. To unify these different groups, everyone who was part of the Roman Empire was required to offer sacrifice to the emperor.

The various peoples of the empire were not required to give up their gods or their traditional religion, but they were required to sacrifice to the emperor as a sign of ultimate allegiance to Rome. To fail to sacrifice to the emperor was, therefore, an act of treason.

This was precisely why Christians were dealt with so harshly by Rome. Although they were in all other ways model citizens, their refusal to give their primary allegiance to the state could not be tolerated—if Christians were given an exemption, it would have to be given to other groups as well.

Plato

Most of the time, governments do not regulate the family too heavily because it can cause deep resentment among its citizens. But political philosophers have always known that loyalty to one's family can result in incomplete loyalty to the state.

Plato recognized that marriage and the family divide a person's loyalty to the state. Thus, when he designed his ideal state, which is described in *The Republic*, he did away with marriage and the family as we know it.

In *The Republic*, Plato envisioned that wives and children should be held in common. To ensure the birth of the next generation of citizens, the state would host a festival to encourage temporary marriages and the begetting of children. This would be done with eugenics in mind, which Plato describes with shocking cruelty:

> But then our rulers must be skillful physicians of the State, for they will often need a strong dose of falsehood in order to bring about desirable unions between their subjects. The good must be paired

with the good, and the bad with the bad, and the offspring of the one must be reared, and of the other destroyed; in this way the flock will be preserved in prime condition.*The Republic* (p. 68).

By the way, it is interesting to note that Plato recommends that the government use deception to make their citizens think they were assigned their temporary spouse by pure chance, while in truth the government would arrange the pairings.

Marriage festivals will be celebrated at times fixed with an eye to population, and the brides and bridegrooms will meet at them; and by an ingenious system of lots the rulers will contrive that the brave and the fair come together, and that those of inferior breed are paired with inferiors— **the latter will ascribe to chance what is really the invention of the rulers**. Plato. *The Republic* (p. 68).

I wonder how often we think we are acting freely while in reality we are being "guided" by our leaders.

Be that as it may, child rearing in Plato's ideal state would not be at the hands of the parents, but in the control of the state. The children of the high quality individuals would be taken away and raised by nurses. Care was to be taken to ensure that the parents never recognize which children belong to them. This would ensure that children would have only one loyalty—loyalty to the state.

Totalitarian Governments
Fortunately, no country has ever attempted to put Plato's ideal state into practice, but some totalitarian governments have tried to drive a wedge into families. The two most obvious examples are Nazi Germany and Soviet Russia.

Nazi Germany

In some ways, Nazi Germany was actually more family friendly than the US government. National Socialist propaganda promoted marriage and having large families. There were also financial inducements to have more children. They even gave a medal, the Cross of Honor of the German Mother, to women who had four or more children. The government also discouraged things that were viewed as being anti-family, such as birth control, homosexuality, and divorce.

But don't think that the National Socialist Party was purely benevolent toward families. The reason for discouraging divorce and encouraging large families was ultimately to strengthen the Party. If parents did not enroll their children in the Hitler Youth or if they were found to be otherwise nonconformist, their children could be removed and placed in a "politically reliable" home.

Soviet Union

While Nazi Germany sought to build up the family to suit its own purposes, the Soviet Union initially tried to weaken marriage. Religious marriage was eliminated and replaced by civil marriage, divorces and abortions became easier to obtain, and single mothers were supported.

The Soviet policy of gradually trying to phase out marriage backfired. By the early 1920s, Russia had seven million homeless children due to the Russian Civil War. The Communist Party realized that its policy was incorrect and began to reverse the trend by encouraging marriage and the family.

The United States

Up until recently, the US federal government played no role in regulating marriage. Regulating marriage fell completely under the laws of the individual states. States were responsible for providing marriage licenses and regulating divorce.

The divorce laws in most states followed the precedents set by English common law. Common law divorce is an adversarial process. That meant that to obtain a divorce, one of the parties had to be at fault—one of the parties had to be guilty of adultery, abandonment, or physical abuse in order for the other spouse to have a cause of action to file for divorce.

No Fault Divorce

Proponents of no fault divorce argued that the law needed to be changed because it subjected the spouses to undue pain and made getting a divorce prohibitively expensive. California was the first state to accept this argument and pass the no fault divorce law in 1970.

While no fault divorce was supposed to make it easier and cheaper for couples to get out of bad marriages, it had some unwanted side effects. The first is that it is responsible for the steep rise in divorce rate over the past 45 years. Now, couples have less incentive to do the hard work of saving their marriage. It is much easier to choose the quick fix of no fault divorce. As an attorney, I've seen lots of cases where women divorce their husband for no other reason than they are bored and believe they will find excitement as a divorcées.

Ironically, by making getting out of marriage easier, it has also encouraged people to be less discerning in selecting a spouse thus increasing the number of bad marriages. After all, why not marry a questionable person if the costs to undoing a mistake are perceived to be low?

A final interesting note about no fault divorce: although it certainly made divorce easier for some couples, especially for childless couples who were only married for a brief time, it failed to make divorce easier for most couples. About 50% of couples are still engaged in conflict five years after they originally file for divorce.

Same Sex Marriage

The landmark Supreme Court case *Obergefell v. Hodges*, which held that there is a fundamental right to same sex marriage, marks the first time that the federal government has gotten involved in regulating marriage.

Advocates of same sex marriage have argued that heterosexual marriages will not be significantly affected by the fact that same-sex couples can marry. I agree. We live across the street from a gay couple. In every way, they are model neighbors. The fact that these two men can now marry has little effect on my own marriage.

But it is not individual gay couples that pose a threat to marriage so much as the legal reasoning that will flow from the *Obergefell* decision.

We've already seen the first effect of the *Obergefell*. Florists, bakeries, and wedding planners who do not want to provide services at gay weddings are being found in violation of anti-discrimination laws. This is true even if the businesses try to claim a religious objection.

The next effect of *Obergefell* that we are likely to see is that the tax-exempt status of any churches and religious schools who oppose same sex-marriage to be challenged. Religious organizations will be faced with the option of either accepting same sex-marriage or seeing a drop off in donations. This will result in a lot of churches, ministries, and schools being closed.

A third effect is that we will likely see more portrayals of same-sex couples in the media, even in media intended for children such as cartoons, and in the public schools. Christian couples who wish to delay the discussion of homosexuality until their children are older will find that they will need to explain these relationships to their children much sooner than they originally planned.

A final effect of *Obergefell* is that it will open the door to further redefinitions of marriage. The same reasoning that has been used to justify the fundamental right to same-sex marriage, can also be used to justify polygamy or polyamory. Will that ever happen? Unless there is a huge shift in the political climate in the US, I believe that it is only a matter of time until we see the first case asking for the "right" of marriage for more than two people.

Social Engineering

Another development we are going to see more of is social engineering that is aimed at children. For example, Fairfax County Public Schools in Virginia, one of the largest and wealthiest school districts in the US, recently approved a curriculum that will teach students about gender fluidity—the concept that everything pertaining to sexual orientation and gender falls within a spectrum.

The effect of teaching impressionable children that their sexual orientation or gender identity falls within a spectrum will only serve to confuse them. It is already happening through the influence of the popular media. A recent British survey revealed that almost half of people between the ages of 18 and 24 identify as something other than 100% heterosexual. It is probable that it will also result in more children identifying as transgender.

While this type of social engineering will probably not have a direct impact on your marriage, it will definitely affect the lives of your children.

Future Changes

In the immediate future, we can expect more social engineering and legislation in support of gender fluidity and transsexual issues. We can also be certain that either polygamy or, more likely, polyamory will be pushed upon society using the government.

Even more ominously, we are now seeing the opening salvos in a war to make pedophilia acceptable. In October 2014, the *New*

York Times published an opinion piece by a legal scholar who argued for pedophilia acceptance using the same line of reasoning that was used to gain public acceptance of homosexuality. How long will it be before we begin seeing pedophile characters on popular TV shows?

Getting Rid of Marriage or Radically Redefining It

In the long term, radical feminists and LGBTQ activists have expressed the desire to do away with institution of marriage altogether. This thought has its basis in Marxism. Frederich Engels viewed the family as the fundamental building block of capitalistic society, which he was trying to destroy. Marriage was, he thought, put into place for the benefit of the "ruling class." He also believed that marriage was inherently oppressive to women:

> "The modern individual family is founded on the open or concealed domestic slavery of the wife, and modern society is a mass composed of these individual families as its molecules." (Frederich Engels, *Origin of The Family, Private Property, and the State*)

Marx and Engels hoped that women entering the work force would destroy marriage. That hasn't happened yet, but there is no question that feminism, with its emphasis on working women, has weakened marriage.

Some feminists have not given up on the idea of doing away with marriage. Feminist Roxanne Dunbar writes that the *coup de grâce* for the family will be delivered by a combination of state sponsored childcare, women in the workforce, and welfare:

> How will the family unit be destroyed? After all, women must take care of the children, and there will continue to be children. Our demand for full-time childcare in the public schools will be met to some degree all over, and perhaps fully in places.

The alleviation of the duty of full-time childcare in private situations will free many women to make decisions they could not before. But more than that, the demand alone will throw the whole ideology of the family into question, so that women can begin establishing a community of work with each other and we can fight collectively. Women will feel freer to leave their husbands and become economically independent, either through a job or welfare. (Roxanne Dunbar, *Female Liberation as the Basis for Social Revolution*)

LGBT activists have been surprisingly open about the ultimate intentions underlying the legalization of same-sex marriage. It is nothing less than an attempt to change the meaning of marriage:

A middle ground might be to fight for same-sex marriage and its benefits and then, once granted, redefine the institution of marriage completely, to demand the right to marry not as a way of adhering to society's moral codes but rather to... radically alter an archaic institution. [Legalizing same-sex marriage] is also a chance to wholly transform the definition of family in American culture. It is the final tool with which to dismantle all sodomy statutes, get education about homosexuality and AIDS into public schools, and, in short, usher in a sea change in how society views and treats us. (Michelangelo Signorile, *Bridal Wave*, Out Magazine (Dec/Jan 1994).

Other feminists/LGTBQ activists appear to be more conflicted about marriage. On the one hand they are happy about it being extended to non-heterosexual arrangements. On the other, they want to eliminate marriage entirely:

I agree that we should have the right to marry, but I also think equally that it is a no-brainer that the institution of marriage should not exist. . . . Fighting for gay marriage generally involves lying about what we're going to do with marriage when we get there, because we lie that the institution of marriage is not going to change, and that is a lie. The institution of marriage is going to change, and it should change, and again, I don't think it should exist. (Masha Gessen, Sydney Writers Festival 2012)

The important thing to stress is that these are not viewpoints held by just a few people. Feminists and Marxists continue to view marriage as "the cornerstone of patriarchy" and a form of sexual servitude against women. Contemporary feminist Meagan Tyler writes:

> The history of marriage in the West is a dark one. European marriage was, historically, a contract endorsed by the state in which a man gained control and rights over a woman and their children, who were seen as little more than goods and chattels. In fact, the institution of marriage was built upon the contractual 'partners' being unequal. (Meagan Tyler, *Death of marriage the path to equality*)

Note that Tyler is not just criticizing marriage as it existed in the past—even modern marriage is inherently unequal:

> Yet we live in a country where the vast majority of women take their husband's name after marriage and take on an even more disproportionate share of the housework after the wedding. So labels of male ownership and the appropriation of women's labour are still alive and well. (Meagan Tyler, *Death of marriage the path to equality*)

Tyler acknowledges that while it might be helpful to "reform" marriage, the best approach is just to do away with it: "Opting out of marriage altogether will provide a quicker path to progress, as only the death of marriage can bring about the dawn of equality for all."

How Seriously Should We Take This?

There are some feminist apologists who defend these radical statements in two ways. First, they say that the authors really didn't mean to imply that they would like to see marriage go the way of the dodo; they only wanted marriage to change to accept same-sex couples.

This defense doesn't hold water. If you read the above statements, it is clear that while they favor same-sex marriage, they are, at the same time, not fond of marriage. They'd be just as happy to see the whole thing go away.

The second defense is that only a few people hold these radical views. Certainly, the vast majority of people who changed their avatars to the LGBTQ rainbow flag after the *Obergefell* decision was handed down do not want to eliminate marriage. They only thought they were supporting marriage equality. But these people are not the thought leaders of feminism or the LGBTQ movement—and at least some of these leaders *do* want to get rid of marriage.

To most people, this talk of radically redefining or eliminating marriage and the family sounds ludicrous. After all, most people today still want to get married. How seriously should we really take this?

The answer is that while this stuff seems outlandish, we ignore it to our own peril. We should be grateful to these activists for expressing their intentions so clearly. It would be a mistake to take them as hyperbole or dismiss them as ravings. These are highly intelligent individuals who have taken their thinking to its logical conclusion. Therefore, *we should take their expressed intention of eliminating marriage very seriously.*

Tying It All Together

The family is under attack on numerous fronts. Consumerism encourages us to constantly work harder in a never-ending quest to accumulate more stuff. Feminism has taught women that they have no value as wives and mothers, but only as corporate drones in the workplace. Companies have joyfully accepted the windfall of a higher supply of workers.

No fault divorce, which was introduced to take some of the acrimony out of divorce, has instead increased the rate of divorce. Men are increasingly avoiding marriage because they fear that that they might be subject to a divorce for no other reason than that their wives are bored. And it is doubtful that divorces are less acrimonious than they were before the advent of the no fault regime.

Meanwhile, feminists and LGBTQ activists have successfully used the government to drive changes to marriage laws and education even without popular support. We can be assured that drumbeat for social change will continue.

How do we fight these changes? One way is through political action—voting for candidates that support traditional marriage. But we have to be honest at this point: this approach has proven woefully disappointing. "Conservative" politicians have a nasty habit of campaigning one way, but governing as liberals once they are elected. But the problem is deeper. The greater part of modern society no longer wants traditional marriage. Thus, getting anything changed through the democratic process is difficult.

However, despite this bleak outlook, the only thing that can truly destroy marriage is if husbands and wives succumb to these attacks. Only we can allow consumerism to drive a wedge into our marriage. While we may not control what our public schools teach about the family, we have the power to believe as we please and to educate our children with our values. We have the ability choose to work on our marriage instead of succumbing to the temptations of *Eat, Pray, Love*. We can swim against the current. Ultimately, the future of marriage rests in *our* hands.

But to keep our marriages together, we'll have to avoid the biggest mistake: divorce.

4. The Truth About Divorce

Attitudes towards divorce have changed in our society. We've gone from viewing divorce as a disaster to be avoided to considering it as a way to empower ourselves. The messages we receive from our culture on divorce are pervasive and powerful.

The Myth of the Enchanting Post Divorce Life

In the past divorce was considered a tragedy. It signified not only the end of a marriage, but also the death of a family. Lives were forever changed—usually in unfavorable ways. As a result, divorce was historically frowned upon. Society wasn't accepting of divorced people. Many divorcees felt a certain shame about the end of their marriage and struggled to reintegrate into society. There were social stigmas for both the divorcees and their children. And this stigma extended to houses of worship. The Catholic Church is probably most famous for its hard line stance against divorce.

Lots of people felt that frowning upon divorce was uncharitable. After all, people make mistakes. Why should society "punish" someone who got divorced?

Myths That Encourage Divorce

To remedy this, our society has given divorce an all out image makeover. Any previous negative associations with the word "divorce" have been wiped clean and replaced with positive ones such as "empowered," "strong," and "free."

Divorce is now a standard fixture of books, television shows, and movies. It is no longer treated like a death of a family. On the contrary, divorce is treated as a healthy way to get rid of a relationship that has outlived its usefulness. This change in attitude is reflected in the real world: nearly half of U.S. marriages now end in divorce. Divorce is quickly becoming the norm.

Here are some of the new cultural messages about divorce:

Divorce Is a Spiritual Awakening

If you pay attention to pop culture you'll see the results of the brilliant metamorphosis that divorce has undergone. Books, television shows, and movies often portray divorce as a spiritual awakening. According to this narrative, filing for divorce enables you to enter a magical nirvana where you will learn deep spiritual truths that you could not have discovered otherwise. The book *Eat, Pray, Love* embodies this type of thinking.

Eat, Pray, Love is about an American woman who leaves her husband and her successful life in a quest to find herself. She takes a year to live in three different cultures. In Italy, she learns about enjoying the material world. In India, she learns about genuine spirituality (of course, everyone knows that Christianity has nothing worthwhile to teach regarding spirituality). Finally, in Bali, she finds true love in the arms of Brazilian businessman.

Sensible people know that while international travel might be fun, one is unlikely to find any sort of enlightenment or long-lasting romance in undertaking it. Despite this, *Eat, Pray, Love* was an immensely popular book that continues to be a powerful influence on countless women. I personally know a woman who, after reading the book left her American husband to travel to South America in search of new age spirituality. In imitation of the *Eat, Pray, Love* heroine, she even found a Brazilian lover whom she later married. Unfortunately, he turned out to be physically abusive so she had to divorce him. Perhaps the book should carry the disclaimer: "Results not typical. Individual results may vary."

Divorce Is a Celebration

In the past, divorce was perceived as something to be sad about. People looked upon the divorce as a personal failure. Today, divorcees, especially female divorcees, are encouraged to take a more celebratory approach to the dissolution of their marriage.

Newly divorced women are celebrating the death of their marriages with "divorce parties," which are sort of like a Quinceañera or debutant ball for grown women.

Divorce parties can vary, but they essentially celebrate freedom from one's spouse and the beginning of a new life. These parties often come with divorce cakes. These cakes are similar to wedding cakes, except that instead of being topped with husband and wife figurines, they are adorned with disturbing cake toppers of grooms being run over by trucks or decapitated by their newly single brides. The divorcees who attend these parties wear t-shirts emblazoned with phrases like "Life Begins at Divorce," "I'm Not with Stupid Anymore," and "The Ex Wives Club."

Divorce Leads to the Sex-filled Single Life

Another popular message that helps encourage people to get a divorce is the idea that singles lead lives filled with nonstop, thrilling sexual escapades. Although this message is a recurring theme in television shows, books, and movies, the most egregious and influential example is *Sex in the City*.

Sex in the City was one of the most influential television shows in history. It ran from 1998 to 2004, but it continues in reruns to this day. Virtually every woman I have ever met has, at one time or another, been a fan of the show.

The reason that *Sex in the City* was so successful in subverting the morality of modern women is that it put an attractive and glamorous face on what is, at its root, an ugly lifestyle.

The plot of *Sex in the City* is simple. It is the story of four single women in their thirties and forties who are living in New York City. They have lots of sex with lots of different, interesting men: authors, artists, dancers, models, businessmen, and scientists. They go to lots of interesting parties and they always seem to have money left over to purchase the most cutting edge fashions of the day.

Despite the fact that their romantic lives are failures, hopping from one meaningless affair to another, the characters are invariably happy. By the end of the series, the women—with one exception that I will discuss below—are happily married. The implication is that one's past does not matter. A person can move from a "fun" promiscuous lifestyle to being happily married as easily as flipping a light switch.

The big lessons taught by *Sex in the City* can be summarized as follows:

1. Single people have more fun, glamorous, and interesting sex than married people.
2. At anytime you please, you can get off the single life sex carousel and get happily married with no detrimental side effects.

While the popular media portrays the single life as a wild sex party, the reality is that married people have *more* sex than singles—up to 50% more. The reason for this is obvious: even the most attractive and desirable person has to put in some effort to find a sex partner. If you have standards, it becomes even harder. The reality is that if you want to have lots of sex, you are better off keeping your current spouse.

The Myth of Perpetual Youth

Sex in the City provided us with one more message—when it comes to being sexually desirable, age does not present any sort of impediment. The one character that was not married by the end of the show, "Samantha," was the oldest of the four *Sex in the City* characters.

The reason that Samantha chooses not to marry is because even though she is in her late forties or early fifties, she still has no problem attracting handsome young men.

Another example is the Bravo channel's series called the *Girlfriend's Guide to Divorce*. The protagonist is a writer in her late forties whose marriage goes south against her will. Of course, the very first time she goes out as a single woman, a handsome young bartender hits her on as soon as she walks into the bar.

Hollywood has even coined a catchy phrase to describe older women who date younger men: the cougar phenomenon. However, even in Hollywood, cougar relationships tend not to last. Demi Moore, possibly the most famous cougar, managed to marry Ashton Kutcher, a man who was sixteen years her junior. At the time, the relationship was lauded as a victory for womankind—at last women could be just like men and date younger paramours. But in the end the pair divorced amidst cheating rumors on Ashton's part. And Ashton, who previously had no children, promptly entered into a relationship with a younger woman, Mila Kunis, who later became the mother of his first child. So much for the feminist victory.

What this boils down to is the idea that we are blessed with perpetual youth. This idea is destructive on many levels. For the young, it promotes wasting time or pursuing careers in lieu of committed relationships and marriage. For young women this is particularly insidious because it advocates delaying childbirth in exchange for the promise of a fulfilling career.

For young men, the lie of perpetual youth encourages promiscuity and a lack of direction. Instead of working toward goals, securing finances, finding a high quality wife, and starting a family, it encourages them to fear commitment and to live as perpetual adolescents.

For older women, the lie that age does not matter is even more destructive. The hard truth is that men find younger women more attractive. The reason is biological. Men are hardwired to be attracted to women who are fertile, but a woman's peak fertility is in her early twenties. Practically speaking, this means that women in their late thirties and beyond are going to have a harder time in attracting a quality mate. This is directly contrary to the message that society would have us believe.

Although older men do not have exactly the same biological constraints that women have, divorce is not a good solution for them either. In the past, women were attracted to a man with financial resources, something that older men usually have more of than young men. But our culture's worship of youth has changed that. Popular Neomasculinity author Roosh Valizadeh wrote:

> We now live in a time where girls in their prime don't care about a man's resources. That trend is spreading to more traditional parts of the world, which means women will start to place more value in exciting metrosexual clowns than mature men with ample means.

In other words, older men should think twice before dumping their wives in the hopes of "upgrading to a younger model." It is more easily said than done.

The way this myth of perpetual youth hurts marriage is obvious—it lulls us into thinking that we have an infinite amount of time. We always have time to go through a painful divorce, pick up the pieces, and fall in love again. Unfortunately, like all these other modern myths, it is not true.

Single Life Is More Interesting

Our current culture glorifies single life as being exciting while painting marriage as dull drudgery and married couples as embittered fuddy-duddies. To see this, you merely need to turn on the television or head to the nearest movie theater and observe the portrayals of singles versus married couples. Singles are able to sit on a sofa and have witty and funny conversations with other singles. They are able to do interesting things. They are able to travel, go to museums, and experience romantic adventures.

Married couples, on the other hand, are often pictured as harried. If couples have children, the children are almost invariably smarter than their parents. Fathers especially are portrayed as bumbling dolts. It's easy to see how married couples that are bombarded with these messages might develop the idea that being married is an impediment to leading a more interesting life.

The Chance to Feel the Thrill of Infatuation Again

The most thrilling time in a romantic relationship is usually at the very beginning. It is the thrill of meeting a new person that we are attracted to, and who may reciprocate our affection. It is a mixture of lust, attraction, hope, anxiety, and, perhaps in some cases, obsession. The feeling can literally cause your heart to pound. This feeling is called *infatuation*.

People mistake infatuation for love, but infatuation is not love. It is possible to become wildly infatuated with a person that you barely know, but true love only comes with knowledge of the other person.

However, infatuation can serve a valuable purpose. It leads us to close off other options so that we can get to know the object of our affections. It can lead us to make heroic changes in our lives. And it can be the gateway to the development of true love.

But many modern people don't treat infatuation as a means to an end. They make it an end in itself. They become addicted to the intoxicating rush that infatuation provides. There are people who actually can waste a lifetime going from one relationship to another always trying to get another infatuation fix. Some of the "commitment phobia" that we see today is the result of people being addicted to infatuation.

If you want to see a testimony to the power of infatuation, observe the continued popularity of the Hollywood romantic comedy genre. These movies, which are usually poorly written, poorly acted, and generally not funny, are perpetual favorites with female moviegoers because they focus on the thrill of infatuation.

People who get married have generally realized that the "high" that infatuation gives is fleeting—or otherwise they would still be on the dating merry-go-round. But that doesn't mean that we don't occasionally miss the adrenaline rush of infatuation. The desire to recapture that rush no doubt accounts for many affairs.

The people who create our movies and television programming are aware of this desire that people have for infatuation. Much of this fare is targeted at women, perhaps because women find the romance that is inherent in a blossoming relationship particularly appealing. Whatever the reason, the media portrays divorce as a chance to again experience infatuation.

The movie *Nights in Rodanthe* takes this message of divorce leading to infatuation to a new level. Not only is the middle aged divorced woman able to find a new lover, but her new boyfriend is also gigantic upgrade over her ex-husband.

The divorcee, played by Diane Lane, owns a bed & breakfast on the beach in Rodanthe, North Carolina. She "bravely" rejects her ex-husband's request to reconcile. Her reward from the universe is that the next guest at her B&B turns out to be a handsome, wealthy, and brilliant doctor played by Richard Gere. The doctor is a humanitarian that puts Mother Theresa to shame, but he is carrying emotional baggage that only the divorcee's love can heal.

The theme of *Nights in Rodanthe* is that divorce is the gateway to meeting that attractive stranger who will rekindle the fires of passion in our lives. While that is possible, it is more likely that divorce will lead to a difficult, romance-free life—but you'll rarely see a movie about that.

Technology Makes It Easy to Find Love

A final message from our culture is that technology now makes it easy to find a new romantic partner. Many singles rely on social media and the countless dating websites and apps available on the market to find love. And with apps like Tinder growing in popularity, one can be fooled into thinking that finding a new partner will be a breeze.

While dating websites and apps can save time in terms of finding other singles, it would be a mistake to think that this is an easy path. In the real world, attraction relies on many factors that we call "chemistry." For reasons we do not entirely understand, we may find ourselves attracted to that woman or man with less than perfect features. Maybe it is the sound of their voice, the way they smile, or the way they carry themselves. While we don't know what magic is behind "chemistry," it is certain that it can't be communicated over a computer or an iPhone.

Users of dating sites and apps like Tinder are reduced to looking at personal profiles and pictures to determine a match. In this environment, it is natural for people to set their standards high, and that means that they will screen out people that they would be attracted to if they met them in real life.

The net effect of this selectivity is that dating apps that rely on pictures and statistics about height, weight, and earning potential, are almost useless for those who don't fit the desired requirements. I've talked to plenty of divorced men who are perpetually ignored on these dating sites because it seems every woman wants a 6'2", devastatingly handsome millionaire. Women, on the other hand, have complained that Tinder's approach of discarding undesirable partners by "swiping left" based solely on appearance is unfair and another way of objectifying women.

By the way, if you happen to be a man and you are tempted to use social media to start an affair, think again. After the hack of the notorious, adultery-encouraging website, Ashley Madison, it was revealed that the site's membership was almost entirely male. Not only does using these sites expose you to potential blackmail, it probably will not deliver on its promise of a "no-strings" affair.

The Reality of Divorce

The Effect of Divorce on Spouses

While our culture paints a rosy picture life after divorce, the reality for most divorcees is not as glamorous as our culture claims. Divorce is one of the most significant destroyers of wealth. A bad divorce can drag on for years. Legal fees, time away from work, therapy bills, and expenses associated with relocating all drain finances. Any equity that the spouses built together will be (at least) halved and prospects for retirement will also have to be reevaluated.

The emotional and physical damage that a divorce inflicts on the spouses is even worse. There is a tremendous amount of stress involved. If you ever happen to catch a celebrity who seems like they have aged ten years overnight, a bit of investigating usually reveals that they have recently gone through a divorce.

The Effect of Divorce on Parents

Divorce is even worse for parents. Being a parent is hard with a partner, but it is absolutely exhausting as a single parent. Again, popular culture lionizes single parents, especially single mothers. We are told that all single moms are strong and independent to the point of being almost superhuman. Some go so far as to say that being a single mother is *better* for children that a married mother. Katy Chatel wrote in the *Washington Post* that being a single mom lets her devote herself to motherhood:

> For me, being the best mother I can be means being a mom alone, at least for now. I want to

devote myself to motherhood, something I fear I can't do with the additional demands of a partnership. Romantic relationships can occupy a lot of mental and emotional energy. I'm not sure I could balance being both a solid partner and mother right now.

Single motherhood also eliminates the stress and complications that arise from incompatible parenting approaches and values in a two-parent home. Thinking of my friends and acquaintances with inadequate partners, I wonder why more people don't choose single motherhood. Parenting alone allows me to make the best decisions for my son without needing to compromise for a partner's differing personal beliefs, needs or career demands.

Of course, this is nonsense. Being a solid husband or wife in no way detracts from your ability to be a good parent. This attitude also ignores the downsides of being a single parent. Single parents burn out fast. The physical, emotional, and financial demands are enough to bring the strongest individual to their knees.

Dealing with your ex can make being a single parent even more difficult. First, there is no guarantee that your ex will step up to the plate financially after the divorce. A parent who refuses to pay child support can plunge a single-family household into poverty.

This can lead to devastating financial problems ranging from making ends meet on a day-to-day basis to affecting the quality of education that the children receive. I know a couple that had their children in one of the most prestigious private schools in the country, but once they divorced it was impossible to pay the tuition. The mother had no choice but to put her children in public school. The previously well-adjusted children developed academic and emotional problems as a result of the change.

Second, divorce causes the children to lose the benefit of having a uniform parenting style. For example, some non-custodial parents treat their visitation days like free-for-alls, completely undoing any structure or balance that the other parent has created. This often leads to one parent getting unfairly labeled as being "mean" or "strict" by the children, while the other gets taken advantage of. To "win over" their children, many parents try to become their children's "best friends," a situation that may alleviate parental guilt, but ends up harming the children.

The Effect of Divorce on Children

Children who go through a divorce will also have to deal with their own anger and sadness over the breakup of their family. This often manifests as behavioral changes, mood swings, and struggles in school.

Some of the effects are very subtle and the children may not even be aware of them until much later in their lives. My own case is a good example of this. My parents divorced when I was seven and my real father was largely absent from my life after that. Although I couldn't express it at the time, I really missed the approval of my father. This led me to feverishly overachieve, accumulating accolades, certifications, and degrees in a perverse attempt to gain the approbation that I had missed. It wasn't until I was well into adulthood that I realized why I was doing some of these silly things.

Probably the most common excuse that parents use to divorce is that if the parents are not happy together, the children will sense it and they will be unhappy as well. However, there is now an overwhelming body of research that indicates the opposite: intact families are better for children even if the parents sometimes struggle.

How to Avoid Our Culture's Pro-Divorce Message

So how do you stay married amidst the divorce hype? First, guard your marriage from the negative influences of divorced people, especially the recently divorced. As the old saying goes, misery loves company. It is human nature to justify our own actions so it is natural for divorced people to accentuate the positive aspects of their divorce while downplaying the negative ones.

After one of my wife's co-workers got a divorce, she became a little bit of an "evangelist" for divorce. She boasted to her co-workers (highly unprofessional behavior) about all the sex that she was having now that she was divorced. It was only when she had a more introspective moment that she confessed that the sex amounted to men merely using her as a human Fleshlight.

A good friend of mine told me that he thinks divorce was contagious. He lives in an upper-class suburban neighborhood. He noted that in the course of three years, every house on his street, except his own, fell victim to divorce. In every case, the wife initiated the divorce. None of the cases involved adultery on the husband's part—to a man, they were all blindsided when their wives filed for divorce.

The reason for the divorce epidemic was that the newly divorced women were negatively influencing the other stay-at-home moms. They regaled the married women with tales of their exciting post-divorce lives. The married women then compared it to what they currently had—a "boring" husband who worked hard providing for his family—and determined that the grass was greener on the other side. These women threw away their marriages and the happiness of their children in the vain hope of achieving a glamorous life.

The second step is avoiding the subtle anti-marriage and pro-divorce messages pumped out by the popular media. This is difficult to do because it is pervasive in television, novels, movies, and popular magazines.

The best way is to avoid this anti-marriage propaganda entirely by consuming less of it. Most movies and television shows are so poorly written and produced that it is a waste of time for anyone with an IQ above 50. By spending less time viewing entertainment you will save money and free up your time to do more productive things.

Some parents I know are very dedicated to protecting their families from all of the corrosive messages of the popular media. Often, they don't own a television, or if they do, it is something they only watch once a month as a special treat.

My wife and I have adopted a less draconian approach. We limit ourselves to watching only a couple of shows a week. It's all about selecting programming that is bigger on entertainment than indoctrination. For example, the HBO series *Girls*, which was created by Lena Dunham, is obviously going to be a vehicle to promote a promiscuous lifestyle.

Even for those few shows and movies that we do watch, we still watch with awareness for the messages that are being pushed. *Game of Thrones*, another popular HBO series based on the novels by George R.R. Martin, clearly has an axe to grind with gay behavior. Where the books are almost entirely silent about gay activity, the television intersperses gayness liberally. As long as you are aware of what the producers are trying to achieve, it is easier to dismiss the message without any ill effect.

Be careful with this approach, though. Some of the anti-marriage and anti-family messages can be very subtle.

Tying It All Together

At some point, American culture went from being overwhelmingly supportive of marriage and the family to subtly undermining it. It does this primarily through the popular media's messages that portray single life as being fun, liberating, and exciting, while portraying married life as being boring, suffocating, and unrealistic.

The anti-marriage animus is so pervasive that it is impossible to extricate yourself from it entirely. There are some things that will help inoculate your marriage from being affected by the divorce-happy culture.

1. **Think independently and swim against the current.** This is what preserved the marriage of my friend who lived in the neighborhood where every other family experienced a divorce. Although his wife was friends with many of the women who divorced their husbands, she was smart enough not to identify herself with their marriage dramas.

2. **Minimize the amount of divorce propaganda.** Minimize your consumption of media that glorifies the single life or denigrates marriage. It is also wise to minimize your exposure to recently divorced people or people who are experiencing marital problems. It is easy for their bitterness to spread to others.

3. **Develop awareness.** Always be aware of the messages that come to us whether that is through television, movies, books, or even people. Reading this book will develop your "radar" so that you have awareness of the underlying propaganda.

The chapters that follow will help you to build a strong foundation for your marriage.

5. How to Cheat-Proof Your Marriage

Infidelity is one of the most devastating things that can happen to a marriage. Other transgressions are easily forgiven if there is true repentance and reform. But because infidelity strikes at the most sacred core of the marriage, the pain that it inflicts can last a lifetime. Most marriages don't survive the damage, and the ones that do are forever transformed.

There are countless articles and books that discuss cheating and dealing with the inevitable aftermath. But is it possible to prevent cheating in the first place? The most conservative estimates are that 23% of men and 19% of women cheat on their spouses. Some surveys indicate that the rate could be as high as 50%.

The above statistics only apply to actual physical infidelity—sexual relations with someone other than your husband or wife. But even more people flirt with cheating by having emotional affairs that can easily ignite and turn into full-blown cheating. What can you do to prevent the venom of infidelity from poisoning your marriage?

Maintain Your Level of Attractiveness

Lots of people think that "letting yourself go" is an option after getting married. I had one obese woman tell me that she felt that her entire life before getting married was one of restriction. She did all sorts of things to maintain a girlish figure before she was married including living on the cabbage soup diet. Marriage, for her, was an opportunity to eat everything in sight. Later, she resented the fact that her husband had lost sexual interest in her, but she was unable to understand why.

If you want to cheat-proof your marriage, you'll want to put down the bag of Cheetos and stop wearing sweat pants. Before you call me a misogynist, let me remind you that this advice is for *both* spouses. It is utterly disrespectful to your husband or wife (and yourself) to let yourself go just because you get comfortable in a relationship.

Don't go to extremes. Starvation is not necessary. You merely need to maintain a basic level of attractiveness by doing the following:

Maintain your weight within the normal BMI range—ideally in the lower half of the range. While the BMI measure is far from perfect, it is a good indicator for most adults. For serious athletes and bodybuilders, the BMI becomes less useful because it doesn't account for the percentage of the body that is muscle, which weighs more than fat.

In addition to maintaining your BMI in a healthy range, all men should do some resistance training. The reason that you need to lift weights is because it is possible to have a normal BMI and still look wimpy and unappealing.

If you need an example of what I am talking about do a Google search on the infamous "Pajamaboy" that the Obama administration used to sell the Affordable Care Act. Pajamaboy probably has an excellent BMI, but he looks like he could not punch his way out of a wet paper bag. This is not the look to strive for if you want to cheat proof your marriage.

Women, too, will want to incorporate a little bit of resistance training into exercise routine for a similar reason. If women do not exercise, it is possible for them to become skinny fat. That is, they may weigh little, but have no shape to their body. Weight training can give women shapely legs, butt, back, and arms while still allowing them to look feminine.

There is no need to go overboard for weight training. The goal for men and women is to have a functional body that looks toned. Giant muscles are not necessary.

Make sure that you are always well groomed. This doesn't mean that you have to wear a tie and a cardigan around the house like Fred MacMurray in the 1950s television show *My Three Sons*. It does mean that even while you are at home, you should have certain standards of appearance.

- Comb your hair.

- Don't wear stained or ratty clothing that has holes in it. Nothing says that you have given up on life more than wearing worn out clothes.

- Wear clothing that fits—no oversize clothing.

- Athletic clothing like sweat pants and yoga pants should be reserved for the times that you are actually doing something athletic. A small change, like wearing a sweater instead of sweatshirt, can make a big difference in how you look and feel.

- Brush your teeth at least in the morning and before bed. Keep your breath fresh the rest of the time as well.

- Shave as appropriate.

You might find it amazing that some married couples omit these basics. People who might be paragons of style during the workweek for their business peers drop their standards on the weekend for the most important person in their life—their spouse.

And don't neglect the little things. Attention to detail often makes the difference between success and failure in life. Take underwear, for example. You might not see a problem with wearing worn-out briefs or panties, but by doing so you are sending a subtle message to your spouse: "I take you, and your sexual attraction for me, for granted."

The importance of maintaining your appearance can be seen in a piece of advice from the manosphere called "dread game." Dread game is a technique used in relationships to make one's partner anxious enough that they fear their lover is about to leave them for another. It can take many forms as long as it instills a sense of doom in your partner. In other words, dread game is making your partner jealous.

One way to use dread game is to keep up your looks so that you can motivate your spouse to look their best too because they will fear losing you. A good illustration of this comes from my old workout partner who is an amateur bodybuilder. He is obviously very fit, but so is his wife. I just assumed that it was because his wife was also interested in physical fitness. But my friend pointed out that the wives of bodybuilders are usually very fit, and he suggested that there is more going on than just a mutual interest in working out.

It turns out that amateur bodybuilders frequently have groupies who follow them to competitions and hang around the gym. This creates a dread game scenario. In order to keep their men faithful, the bodybuilders' wives work at maintaining their level of attractiveness. As the saying goes, a man won't go for a burger if he knows there is filet mignon at home.

I'm not advocating dread game. In its advanced form, dread game involves cultivating a stable of potential romantic rivals to your current spouse. But that involves flirting with others—which is a good way to destroy your marriage. Still, by maintaining your appearance, you signal to your spouse that you value him or her, and that you are someone who is valuable.

Maintaining your appearance is a key part of the foundation of your marriage. However, staying attractive is only a beginning. By itself, it is not enough to keep a marriage cheat proof. I wrote an article on *Return of Kings* about an acquaintance whose wife was contemplating cheating on him even though he looked like he could be on the cover of *Men's Fitness* magazine. To truly cheat proof your marriage, there is a lot more work to do.

Avoid Close Friendships with the Opposite Sex

It's an age-old question – can heterosexual men and women really just be friends? This question has been the topic of countless books, movies, and sitcoms. In the movie *Harry Met Sally*, Harry states, "Men and women can't be friends because the sex part always gets in the way." Personally, I think that a quote from comedian Chris Rock is even closer to the truth:

> Do you know what a platonic friend is to a woman? It's like a dick in a glass case. 'In case of emergency, break glass.'

Is it true that men and women cannot be friends? I've given the matter a lot of thought and I believe the answer, with few exceptions, is 'no.' Men and women cannot be "just friends." And if either party is married and wants to stay that way, then the answer is an even more emphatic 'no.'

I have had friendships with women whom I had no interest in sexually. I would treat them just like I would a male friend, but inevitably I would later learn that the woman wanted more from the relationship.

Of course, it works both ways. In college I had friendship with a girl who probably thought that our friendship was platonic, but the entire time I was hoping that it would turn into something else. Thankfully, I learned quickly never to get into the "friend zone" again, but men and women do it all the time.

I mentioned that there were exceptions to the rule. What are they? The only one I can think of is if the woman is significantly older than the man, and well beyond her child-bearing years, that it is possible to have a safe, platonic friendship. The opposite, where the man is significantly older than the woman, is not true.

But why do married people need to take such a hard line on male/female friendships?

The nature of men. The first reason is the nature of men. An honest man will tell you that he wants two very different things. On the one hand, he will tell you that he wants to be married to one beautiful woman, his true love, for his entire life. He wants to love, honor, and cherish that woman all the days of his life.

On the other hand, the same honest man will tell you that he would also like to have commitment-free sex with lots of different women. There's actually been a development in society that caters to this desire that men have to have sex with no strings attached. It is called *friends with benefits*.

The way the media paints *friends with benefits* is that both sides get exactly what they want. The man and the woman both like each other as friends, and they both enjoy attachment-free sex. They are equal. But the reality is different.

When I talk to men who are in a *friends with benefits* relationship, they universally regard the woman as an object, and a low value object at that. They regard it as a pleasant diversion until they can score a hotter chick. Also, they typically don't value the woman's friendship very much either. She's just a "fuck buddy"—nothing more.

A woman who is in a *friends with benefits* relationship usually views it differently. She secretly hopes that the combination of friendship plus sex is going to make the man realize what a great girl she is and upgrade her status from "fuck buddy" to girlfriend. It almost never happens.

So all men have these contradictory desires. The wholesome desire is to be committed for life to one woman. The other desire is to have commitment free sex. Good men are smart enough to realize that the lifetime commitment will yield greater happiness so they discipline themselves to remain faithful to one woman.

But the temptation is always there, and even good men can crumple if the temptation is overwhelming. A friend who is a priest told me that he had a wise spiritual director while he was in seminary. On one occasion he asked his spiritual director when he could relax his guard against sexual temptation. His spiritual director replied, "one second after you die."

Of course, not all men are good. Some will, when presented with the opportunity, take advantage of a female friend. I am personally aware of men who deliberately target married women, and their approach is to get the married woman to lower her guard by feigning friendship. It is just better to avoid the potentially dangerous situation all together.

The nature of women. The other reason for married people to avoid friendships with the opposite sex is the nature of women. Women, contrary to what our culture says, do not want commitment free sex. Even when they are having affairs, sex is usually within the context of a relationship. But I had the misfortune of learning first hand that women can be very political—even devious—in their dealings with men.

In my first job after college I had a female boss who was just a couple of years older than me. She quickly befriended me, and told me a lot of personal things, including the fact that her husband was cheating on her. At the time, I thought she was just confiding in me as a friend, but later she invited me to sleep at her house over the weekend while her husband was away with the implication that more would happen than just sleep. Naturally, I demurred saying that I didn't think it would be appropriate. That sent her into a rage from which our professional "friendship" never recovered.

I don't think my boss wanted to have sex with me because I was some sort of super handsome Adonis—I think she merely wanted to use me to get back at her husband. Or, giving it a better spin, she wanted to use me as a fallback to her failing marriage. Whatever the case, we both would have been better off if our relationship had remained strictly professional.

Of course, not all male/female relationships end in sex, but even here, it can be a dangerous distraction. Women often use platonic relationships with men as emotional crutches. It's a selfish way acquiring male attention. But even an emotional affair is something that you should avoid if your goal is to stay married.

How to treat male/female relationships. At the time of Jesus, there was a sect of Pharisees called the "Blind" or "Bruised and Bleeding Pharisees." They earned their name because of their practice of looking at the ground to avoid looking at women, who could be a source of temptation. Because they were often looking at the ground, they would bump into things thus earning the epithet, "Bruised and Bleeding." It is possible that Jesus had this particular sect in mind when he called the Pharisees "blind guides."

There is no need to go to the extremes of the Bruised and Bleeding Pharisees. In fact, it is not possible to function in the modern world without men and women interacting with each other. But it is possible to have pleasant and warm relationships with women without the danger of close friendship. The key is to be *friendly but not familiar.* Here are some ways to do it:

- Avoid spending unnecessary time alone together. When you have the option, include your spouse, a third party, or meet in a public place in full view of others.

- Keep the conversation friendly and professional. Don't discuss irrelevant personal concerns.

- Don't make references to the way the other person looks. As a married person, you really don't have any reason to compliment a person of the opposite sex on their appearance. Compliments on their work are acceptable.

- Don't flirt or initiate any sort of excessive contact.

Of course, in all your dealings with the opposite sex, you should never act awkwardly or draw attention to the fact that you are trying to maintain distance. It should be so perfectly natural that the other person never realizes that you are keeping a professional distance.

Don't Believe the 80/20 Rule of Relationships

There is another modern myth that is making the rounds from relationship experts. Like all myths, it is based on a partial truth. The myth, called the 80/20 rule of relationships, states that in a healthy romantic relationship, people only get 80% of what they want from their partner. The other 20% are needs that cannot be met by their partner. Relationship "experts" posit that the reason that people cheat is because they are not getting this 20% of needs fulfilled. If you get your needs met through some other healthy relationships, the experts say, you will never feel the need to stray.

How do you fulfill this supposed 20% of needs? The "experts" say that you should find other people, including people of the opposite sex, to meet these needs. Does your spouse not compliment your appearance? Well then, you should find a friend who does make you feel attractive. And if this friend happens to be of the opposite sex, then that's not really a problem.

At first glance the 80/20 rule seems reasonable. No one is perfect so it would make sense that your spouse could not conceivably fulfill 100% of your needs. We are all social creatures so one person will not fulfill all of our needs and interests. For example, I really enjoy reading philosophy, theology, and political theory. My wife has very little interest in those topics so if I want to have a meaningful discussion about them; I have to talk to friends who share those interests.

The problem arises when the needs a husband or wife does not meet are emotional or sexual needs. If you think that your wife finds you unattractive, this is something to discuss with your wife. It indicates there is something amiss in your relationship. Trying to find an outside relationship to cure this problem would be a giant mistake.

So the 80/20 rule is partially true: your spouse will not be able to be all things to you—it would be irrational to even think that they should. However, the 20% of "needs" that your spouse does not meet are also relatively unimportant in comparison to the 80% that your spouse does meet. In the case of my interest in philosophy, it is not the end of the world if I don't have anyone to talk to about it. In other words, those 20% of "needs" are not really needs at all. They are merely "nice to haves."

In short, don't be bamboozled by the advice of the supposed relationship experts. Work on your relationship with your spouse for the things that are the most important to you. But there is no compelling reason that you need to start opposite sex friendships to fulfill other desires. There is a much better way—same sex friendships.

Make Wholesome Same Sex Friendships

While friendships with the opposite sex can present temptations to infidelity, same-sex friendships can be a wholesome outlet to engage in interests that we do not share with our spouse. Same-sex friendships provide all the benefits of camaraderie without the awkwardness and sexual tension that can accompany opposite sex friendships.

In today's culture, it is very difficult for men to form wholesome relationships with other men. Catholic priest Father John McCloskey has written about how it is still common for Italian men to get together as a group to have lunch and enjoy each other's company:

> Not too long after a glorious liturgical event in St. Peter's Square, I went out to lunch in the Piazza Navona with several American couples. During our conversation and enjoyment of Italian pasta, I took a close look at the next table. There was a group of seven or eight Italian men who were eating, drinking vino rosso, and engaging in boisterous conversation, clearly enjoying themselves. I got the impression that this was not a singular event but rather one of frequent meetings of long-time close friends. (Fr. John McCloskey, *Friendship: The Key to the Evangelization of Men*)

But Fr. McCloskey observes that it has become increasingly difficult for American men to spend time in the company of other men. Virtually every traditional bastion of male-only companionship has been destroyed by feminism. Men's clubs have been forced to include women because failure to do so results in accusations of being discriminatory toward women. Sporting events, which used to be largely male affairs, now contain an even mix of men and women. And men now avoid getting together for a simple dinner for fears of being mistaken for being gay:

> To complicate matters still further, in today's society many male relationships are openly homosexual... Many forms of public entertainment—films, television, and the theater—have accepted homosexuality as normal, and begun to portray heterosexual males as fools who live under the sway of domineering women. One of the many unhappy side-effects of this open public perversion is the fact that when any small group of adult males is seen together, at least in some urban centers, they are assumed to be

homosexuals. (Fr. John McCloskey, *Friendship: The Key to the Evangelization of Men*)

Women do a lot better on this point because it is still socially acceptable for women to go out shopping or to share a lunch. Brunch "with the girls" can be a great opportunity to talk about things that your husband does not share an interest in.

Same-sex friendships provide another benefit: They can serve as a spur for us to achieve more in our lives. Once a month I get together with a group of men for breakfast. As I learn about everything that these men are doing in their lives, their example serves as a goad for me to be a better husband and father.

While same-sex relationships can be great ways to have fun, recharge, and learn new things, they can be abused. If your "girls night out" is just an excuse to get drunk, it is an unhealthy relationship that you would be better off without. Ditto if your "evening with the guys" ends up at a strip club. And even when the relationship is a wholesome one, if it wastes time, it is a bad idea.

The key to making your same-sex friendships opportunities to uplift you and your marriage is to ensure that you are associating with high quality people. Friends should be chosen with caution and care. The old adage, birds of a feather, flock together, is still good advice.

In short, surround yourself with good influences. In Steve Harvey's book *Act Like a Success, Think Like a Success*, he says, "You should be living your life surrounded by people who are like-minded, service-oriented, and grateful, people who are trying to accomplish things, and who bring something to the table." Your friends should be people who inspire you to be a better person and achieve more in life.

This same mindset should go into choosing those confidants who will influence your marriage. You must surround yourself with people who believe in their vows and who are rooting for you to succeed. This kind of support is essential to staying married.

When it comes to your friends, choose carefully. Avoid anyone who tends to draw you away from your marriage or your faith. Here are some of the types that would make bad bets as a same-sex friend:

- A person who is very critical of his or her spouse or critical of marriage in general.

- Someone who encourages you to spend inordinate amounts of time away from your spouse and family.

- People who encourage you to adopt bad habits such as: drug or alcohol abuse, gambling, or participating in questionable activities.

Surrounding yourself with positive, successful, and moral friends can be a great way to not only engage in interests that your spouse does not have, it can actually serve to strengthen your marriage.

Limit Social Media Use

There is immense power in social media. It can be used to market a business, stay in touch with friends and family, spread news that the mainstream outlets are not covering, and debate important issues. But social media can also be used for a nefarious purpose—using it to find people with whom you can cheat on your spouse.

Using social media to cheat is so common that you probably already know someone whose marriage has been destroyed by a spouse that went on Facebook and used it to hook up with an old flame.

It is not just old flames that you have to worry about. Platforms like Twitter, Instagram, and Facebook are great places to meet new people who share an interest. And if you are not careful, they are also great places to strike up a new romance.

One of the reasons that this happens is that it is so easy to create a false image on social media. People only see pictures, witty comments, and a wide range of interests. They don't see that the person might have a touch of mental illness or a spending problem. They don't see that their new love interest might be a serial philanderer, a lousy parent, or a have drug addiction. They only see the carefully crafted image of what their paramour wants them to see.

I personally witnessed a marriage ended by a wife who found a man on Facebook. He seemed so much more interesting than her husband. The new guy was into yoga, kayaking, luxury sports cars, firearms, martial arts, stock investing, high technology gadgets, weightlifting, running, playing the guitar, jazz, cooking, sailing, gardening, and meditation. In other words, this guy painted himself as James Bond in the flesh. There was no way that her poor husband could compete.

After exchanging text messages and doing Skype chats for a long time, the wife decided to meet with her real life secret agent. He said that he was in a "loveless marriage" (of course) and he professed his undying love for her. It didn't take long before the emotional affair became physical. Predictably, the husband found out about the infidelity and initiated a divorce.

Not surprisingly, James Bond ended the affair and moved on to his next conquest after he became bored. The wife also discovered, too late, that most of this man's accomplishments and interests were ephemeral at best. In reality, he was just a pot-smoking loser who got off on shagging gullible married women.

There are other downsides to social media that do not involve cheating. It encourages status signaling and fame whoring. Like the James Bond guy I just mentioned, there are tons of people out there who are trying to impress you with their interesting lives. If you are not careful, it is easy to begin to think that your life doesn't measure up. It can even make you depressed. A 2010 study by the University of Leeds found that "over-engaging in websites that serve to replace normal social function might be linked to psychological disorders like depression and addiction."

The use of social media also provides wealthy companies such as Facebook with precious information about you and your family that they sell in exchange for advertising dollars. These same companies then turn around and fund political candidates and media campaigns that further lower the moral temperature of society.

If you want your marriage to survive, you and your spouse will need to limit your exposure on social media using some of the following tactics:

Avoid social media entirely. Social media and texting are a recent invention. Not too long ago, it was possible to have a fulfilling life—probably much more fulfilling than our own—without it. Dropping social media use would actually improve the lives of most people. Most social media usage is a gigantic waste of time that would be better spent with your spouse or working on self-improvement.

Not using social media in our day and age sets you apart from the herd, and it is one of the best things you can do to cheat proof your marriage.

Use social media but be open about it. Not everyone can avoid the use of social media. Most of the time, the requirement is business related, but sometimes people use it as a convenient way of staying in touch with family and friends.

Our family is a case in point. My wife is a very private person, so she doesn't use social media. However, since I am a writer, I do use social media to promote my work. However, my wife has access to all my social media accounts so my usage is completely transparent.

My wife hardly ever actually checks my accounts with the exception of my Twitter feed, which she finds entertaining, but it does instill an extra degree of trust in a relationship if you are completely open.

To some people, this may seem like an enormous invasion of individual privacy, but I believe that if my behavior is above board, then there is nothing that I need to hide from my wife.

Even if your spouse has access to your social media accounts, you still have the responsibility of being friendly but not familiar when interacting with members of the opposite sex. This takes some discipline because we are innately curious. Cut off relationships that are starting to become too familiar early before it becomes a true temptation.

Be aware of your spouse's use of social media, texting, and email. I am not recommending that you begin to distrust your spouse—that would be counterproductive. It would only serve to alienate your spouse.

Ordinarily, there is no reason to check your spouse's accounts. Your trust in your spouse should be very high. However, authentic trust is not the same as naïveté. If all of a sudden, your spouse's use of social media or texting suddenly spikes, it is time to start paying attention.

In the case of my friend's marriage, his wife went from spending very little time texting to constantly texting with the "James Bond" guy. Her excuse was that she was doing it for work, and her husband never questioned it. If he had done so, he would have been able to stop the affair long before it became physical. And an emotional affair, while still being a betrayal of trust, is easier to forgive and bounce back from than from infidelity that has been consummated.

These recommendations are definitely counter cultural. Most people bristle at the very suggestion that social media should be avoided. They bristle even more at the suggestion that they need to be transparent with their spouse, but if we are going save our marriages, discipline in this area is mandatory.

Don't Expose Your Spouse to Temptation

I've been a big fan of Arthurian legend ever since I was a kid. There is something about knights in shining armor, jousts, sword fights, and going on quests that appeals to every boy. But there was one part of Arthurian legend that I never liked—the adulterous relationship between Sir Lancelot and Queen Guinevere.

The love affair between Arthur's wife and his greatest knight started even before Arthur and Guinevere were married. According to the story, Guinevere was betrothed to Arthur, and she was looking forward to Arthur picking her up from her father's castle to be taken to Camelot for the wedding ceremony. However, Arthur was busy so he sent his trusted friend to pick up his future wife. It was on the long journey back to Camelot that Lancelot and Guinevere fell in love with each other.

Don't make the same mistake in your own marriage. We tend to become attracted to people that we spend a lot of time with, even if we would not otherwise find them attractive. This likely accounts for a high percentage of affairs because the straying spouse typically bids down—their new paramour is usually a big downgrade from their spouse.

We can't prevent our spouse from spending time with people of the opposite sex at work—that is just a necessary evil—but we can minimize the temptation outside of the workplace:

- **Don't let your spouse spend time alone with your friends.** Friends are often a source of affairs so don't trust them blindly. When I was a kid, my mother's best female friend, who she thought she could trust with her life, propositioned my father. He told my mother, and she ended the friendship.

- **Don't let people of the opposite sex take tasks that you should be doing.** Does your spouse need a ride to the airport? It is better that you juggle your schedule rather than letting your neighbor drive your wife there.

- **Don't let your spouse become close friends with members of the opposite sex.** This rule applies even to the recent fad of married women having "gay boyfriends." This is a gay man who shops with women and acts like "just one of the girls." Women end up completely trusting these gay boyfriends and even undress in front of them. My rule of thumb is that I am not going to let any man spend time alone with my wife, regardless of what sexual orientation they profess.

- **Call each other daily while on business travel.** Business travel can be an enormous source of temptation for men and women. For men, the temptation may take the form of prostitutes. For women, it is more likely to be a coworker.

  My wife and I have an agreement that when I travel, I always call her to say good night before I go to bed. I've never actually been tempted to cheat while I am away from home—it is just a nice reminder for us to reconnect with each other.

None of these measures indicate lack of trust in your spouse. Rather, they are simply ways of ensuring your spouse is not exposed to unnecessary temptation.

Avoid Pornography

Our society is drenched in pornography and other salacious entertainment such as strip clubs. At some point, local law enforcement gave up on enforcing the obscenity laws. Now, with the advent of the internet, the type of porn that used to be reserved for perverts sitting in the back rooms of inner city book stores is streamed into our homes over optic fiber cable.

Even if you avoid watching any internet pornography, television itself has steadily gotten more risqué. Almost all of the best-written television shows now contain a good smattering of nudity and gobs of simulated sex.

It used to be that viewing porn and going to strip clubs was strictly a male thing. But there has been a major effort in the media to tell women that they should imitate men in this regard.

Not too long ago, a bachelorette party was a relatively tame affair that consisted of women getting together and giving the future bride presents such as lingerie. Today, bachelorette parties frequently involve women wearing dildos, getting "shitfaced," and going to clubs to watch male strippers. Sometimes, these events involve genuine infidelity. My wife's hairstylist relayed a story to my wife about a bride who actually had sex with the male stripper at her party. When her fiancé got wind of it, he canceled the wedding.

There has also been a push in the media to encourage women to become porn viewers. This has been a hard sell as women are not naturally inclined to watch porn. It has been reserved to men because we are easily stimulated by a visual image, but the porn industry wants to expand its market. Talk shows and relationship books talk about how watching porn can be empowering for women. While I think they've met with very limited success, some women have been sucked in by the propaganda.

But what is wrong with porn? The media tells us it is a harmless sexual outlet and a healthy way to spice up our romantic life. They are wrong. Pornography damages relationships and ruins lives. Viewing porn on a regular basis sets up unrealistic expectations about sex, bodies, and libido.

One of the ways it does that is through desensitization. Porn allows us to view a wide variety of different sexual partners engaged in sexual acts that bear little resemblance to real sex. In order to become stimulated, viewers of porn have to search for ever more degenerate forms of pornography. There are even men who become unable to perform in real life because natural sex is no longer stimulating enough.

Pornography is also a form of infidelity. While it certainly does not entail the same level of betrayal that an adulterous act with a real person would, it does involve looking for sexual satisfaction from people other than your spouse. It also weakens our will making it more likely that we will seek to act out our infidelity in the real world.

If you want to cheat-proof your marriage, a zero tolerance policy is the best approach toward pornography and other salacious entertainment such as strip clubs.

Develop a Hobby Together

One reason people stray from their marriage is simply because they spend less time with their spouse. In the beginning of most relationships, love-struck couples spend as much time as possible with each other and often have many common interests. But as the years go by and life grows more hectic with children and work, some married couples begin to drift apart.

One way to avoid this is to engage in a common interest or hobby. Whether it's a passion for cooking, ballroom dancing, or exercise, a common interest will help keep a connection with your spouse. In my marriage exercise fills that role. My wife and I regularly workout together either in the gym or by taking long jogs or hikes along the trails near our home.

Make your Marriage a Top Priority

Couples who successfully stay married don't do so because of dumb luck. They actually put a lot of work into their relationship. This means your marriage should be your top priority. No matter how hectic life becomes with work, children, and other stressors, a married couple must make time for each other. Problems arise when your spouse becomes an afterthought at the end of a busy day. Make time each evening for one on one conversation and romance and make it a priority. You can DVR the funny sitcom, basketball game, or news program that's currently on TV. Your spouse comes first.

Remember your Vows

There was a time when a vow was considered sacred and men were taken at their word. The Bible tells us "When you make a vow to God, do not delay to fulfill it. He has no pleasure in fools; fulfill your vow" (Ecclesiastes 5:4). In Arthurian legend, knights were expected to fulfill their vows even if it meant risking their lives.

Our culture has minimized the importance of vows. This coincides with the loss of faith. If God does not exist, vows made to him do not count. Consequently, most people think nothing of breaking their vow when times get tough. Even Christians put little stock in their vows. This amounts to a practical atheism.

One way to reverse this is to set aside a time each week to reflect on what your vows mean to you. It doesn't need to be for more than a minute or two, and it is best done during your regular time of prayer. This simple practice can go a long way in keeping us on track.

Tying It All Together

Although infidelity is common in our culture, it is far from inevitable. The suggestions above can be summarized in the following points:

1. Look your best.
2. Avoid temptation from relationships, social media, and pornography.
3. Don't expose your spouse to temptation.
4. Spend abundant time with your spouse.

Ultimately, the best way to inoculate you and your spouse from cheating is simply to have a healthy, happy marriage. And the foundation to any happy marriage is plenty of romance and sex.

6. How to Keep Romance and Sex in Your Marriage

The primary reason that men get married is for the sex. Sure, we also want companionship, and some men might want children, but it is the promise of regular sex that really closes the deal.

While women are also interested in sex, their reasons for getting married are more varied. One of these reasons is that women are attracted to the romance of marriage. That is why it is ironic that sex and romance are some of the first things to suffer when life starts to get busy.

A successful marriage will include generous amounts of sex and romance. This chapter provides some suggestions to keep passion in your marriage or rekindle it if it has started to wane.

Romance

When we hear the word romance we typically think of ostentatious displays. Rose petals covering a bed surrounded by dozens of unique looking candles. A bottle of Dom Pérignon. Smooth jazz playing softly in the background.

While none of these are bad things (I will pass on the rose petals, candles, and smooth jazz), romance consists more of an attention to detail than ostentatious displays. Here are some ideas on how to inject more romance into your marriage.

Remember important dates. Your spouse's birthday and your wedding anniversary are two dates that must never be forgotten. Make sure that you celebrate them as very special days.

Buy thoughtful gifts for your spouse. For the guys: Your wife wants gifts that you consider frivolous. Jewelry is romantic; a new vacuum cleaner is not. Here are some romantic gift ideas for your wife:

- Jewelry. Be careful to select the style and piece of jewelry that she likes. When we were first dating, I bought my wife a Tiffany necklace. I thought she would have been impressed with the blue box—she wasn't. The necklace didn't match her style. If I had paid more attention, I would not have made that mistake.

- A romantic dinner. A romantic dinner with delicious food is a hit with every woman. If you are a reasonable cook, a homemade dinner can be romantic. If not, substitute a trip to a high quality restaurant.

- A romantic trip. A friend of mine took his wife to Paris to celebrate their anniversary, but it is not necessary to go that far. A picnic in the country (again, with delicious food) fits the bill.

- A day of pampering. Some women love to get pampered with a trip to a spa. But I think most women would also appreciate a massage from their husband.

- Breakfast in bed. Any woman would welcome a surprise breakfast cooked by dad and the children.

Reserve your more practical gift giving such as clothing or appliances to Christmas or as the need arises. By the way, sexy lingerie that you would like your wife to wear does not qualify as a romantic gift for her. It is a gift for you.

Wives have an easier job in buying gifts for their husbands. The gift merely needs to be thoughtful. When buying clothes, pay attention to your husband's preferred style. If you know he is a dedicated Apple bigot, don't buy him a Windows-powered PC. And if he really wants to own a Rolex one day, don't get him a

$100 department store watch. It would be better to save up and get him the real thing.

Surprise your spouse. Surprise your husband or wife with little things. This could be a hand written note conveying your affection, some roses sent to your wife's workplace for no particular reason, or a spontaneous homemade dinner consisting of your spouse's favorite foods. And wives, your husband will always welcome unexpected sex.

Be massively affectionate. Romance is not limited to gifts and vacations, it also involves abundant physical contact. For men, it is easy to get caught in the cycle of only hugging and kissing as a prelude to sex. That's a mistake. Hugging, kissing, and cuddling are an integral part of romance. Don't let a day pass without engaging in physical affection.

Sex

If you are not having sex with your spouse on a regular basis, it could signal that there is a problem. Of course, there may be times that sex just isn't possible, such as right after giving birth, but most of the time, regular sex should be the norm, not the exception.

In most cases, couples don't stop having sex due to some problem in the relationship. The usual reason is that couples are just too busy to find time to have sex. This is often the case when children come into the picture. There is a funny Luvs diaper commercial that has a couple sneaking in sex while their first child takes a nap. After the birth of their second child, the couple is still sneaking, but this time they are trying to grab a quick nap instead of sex while their children are napping.

Even though failing to have sex is usually the result of being too busy, if you allow the sexless condition to continue, it can cause problems. If the husband or wife is not getting sex at home they are more susceptible to sexual advances from a third party.

74

Attitude Toward Sex

A good starting point is that husband and wife should not regard sex as something that their spouse has to earn. Sex is part of what we sign up for when we say, "I do."

This simple truth has really been lost in the past several years because of feminism. Feminist scholar Andrea Dworkin went so far as to suggest that all heterosexual intercourse, including marital intercourse, was rape. Her contention was that sex by its very nature is an act of aggression against a female.

While Dworkin's contention is ridiculous on its face, the sentiment has seeped into our popular culture and into our consciousness. Young women are trained to resent men at some level—it is just something they absorb from merely living in our society.

Choreplay

One manifestation of this resentment is the idea that a man needs to do household chores such as washing the dishes, cleaning, or doing laundry to earn sex from his wife. The concept is called "choreplay" and feminists push it as a way of making the sexes more equal. High-powered Facebook executive Sheryl Sandberg made the case for choreplay in a March 5, 2015 *New York Times* op-ed:

> If that isn't exciting enough, try this: Couples who share chores equally have more sex. As the researchers Constance T. Gager and Scott T. Yabiku put it, men and women who work hard play hard... If [men] want to do something nice for their partners, instead of buying flowers, they should do laundry. A man who heard this was asked by his wife one night to do a load of laundry. He picked up the basket and asked hopefully, "Is this Lean In laundry?" Choreplay is real.

The problem is that Ms. Sandberg only read the abstract of the research by Gager and Yabiku. *The Federalist* reporter Mollie Hemingway dug deeper and discovered that the research actually contradicted Sandberg's conclusion. Gager and Yabiku write:

> Our results do not support the notion that more egalitarian divisions of labor are associated with higher sexual frequency. Instead, we find that households in which men do more traditionally male labor and women do more traditionally female labor report higher sexual frequency. This suggests that among heterosexual couples, the relationship between housework and a couple's sex life is governed by a gendered set of sexual scripts.

In other words, couples that have traditional gender roles actually have more sex. Doing choreplay will result in less sex. It should not come as a surprise because women like manly men.

The Right Attitude

Rather than viewing it as a reward for good behavior, spouses should view sex as a mutual self-giving.

This attitude is exhibited by Michelle Duggar of the TLC reality television show *19 Kids and Counting.* In an interview with NBC television show *Today*, Michelle Duggar said: "In your marriage there will be times you're going to be very exhausted. Your hubby comes home after a hard day's work, you get the baby to bed, and he is going to be looking forward to that time with you."

Her advice to other women is to "be available. Anyone can fix him lunch, but only one person can meet that physical need of love that he has, and you always need to be available when he calls."

Michelle Duggar's advice is biblically based. St. Paul in the first letter to the Corinthians writes:

> The husband should give to his wife her conjugal rights, and likewise the wife to her husband. For the wife does not rule over her own body, but the husband does; likewise the husband does not rule over his own body, but the wife does. Do not refuse one another except perhaps by agreement for a season, that you may devote yourselves to prayer; but then come together again, lest Satan tempt you through lack of self-control. 1 Cor. 7:3-5.

Some modern day preachers seem to think that St. Paul was a sexist, but that is certainly not in evidence in this passage. His advice is perfectly egalitarian: husbands need be available to have sex with their wives just as much as wives need to be available to their husbands.

The only thing I would add here is that we need to be reasonable. We are not machines. There are going to be times when we are going to honestly feel sick, tired, or just not in the mood. In these cases, spouses should be understanding of each other.

Rekindling the Flame

"Well and good," you might say, "but what should we do if we have become distant from each other? How can we rekindle the flame?"

If your married love life has cooled off, a biblical injunction is likely to leave you cold. Ideally, there is more to sex within marriage than pure duty.

To begin reconnecting, the main thing to realize is that sex doesn't start in bed, especially for women. Men often find it easier to switch immediately to sex, but for most women seduction needs to be an ongoing process.

1. Maintain a flirty and playful attitude with your spouse. You don't have to be lewd. Just keep things light hearted.

2. Make a habit of touching your spouse regularly. Frequent hugs and kisses make your husband or wife feel loved. While a hug and a kiss before you leave for work is certainly a good idea, don't forget to include plenty of spontaneous contact. Include frequent cuddling and give your spouse the occasional massage.

3. Show your spouse that you feel passionate about them through words and physical contact. There is a big difference from a robotic "hi honey, I'm home kiss" and a kiss that communicates passion for your spouse. As I mentioned under the "Romance" section, make sure that your marriage includes abundant, affectionate, physical contact.

A second thing that you should do is look for ways to make each other's lives easier. There might be times when the husband will let his wife sleep in so that she is not exhausted, or vice versa. But don't let this degenerate into choreplay. Again, the focus is on mutual self-giving.

Tying It All Together

Romance and sex are indispensible aspects of any successful marriage. If one or both of them is missing, it is a warning signal that you need to work on reclaiming them. In addition to providing a solid foundation for your marriage, romance and sex also make marriage fun.

7. The Role of Attitude in Marriage

Having the right attitude is another part of the foundation of any successful marriage. If you and your spouse adopt the following characteristics your marriage will be able to weather almost any storm.

Positive and Optimistic

Having a positive attitude means that you try to see the best in *any* situation and that you remain open to *all* options for solving problems.

Although I am relentlessly positive nowadays, that wasn't always the case. I have always prided myself as being a "realist." I felt that simply having a positive attitude in the face of adversity was somehow disingenuous. Wouldn't it be better to analyze the problem with cold realism and admit defeat if there were no viable options? What difference would feeling positive make?

It turns out that there is hard scientific research that demonstrates that having a positive attitude does make a difference. Dr. Martin E.P. Seligman of the University of Pennsylvania dedicated over 25 years to researching optimists and pessimists. He found that being optimistic could lead to a better life by defeating depression, boosting the immune system, and helping people become successful.

Having a positive attitude does not mean that you are unfazed when adversity strikes. It simply means that you don't let adversity conquer you. Instead, you try to find what is good about the situation. It also means that you keep a cool head so that you are open to evaluating all the available options. In other words, being positive means putting yourself in the ideal state where you can *creatively* solve problems.

A positive attitude will not just help you with your marriage; it will help you in every area of your life. It is even the key to surviving life and death situations. Even the Boy Scouts recognize that "a positive mental attitude may be the most essential element in survival" if you are lost in the wilderness. It will also help you succeed in business or sports.

The thing that really convinced me of the practicality of a positive attitude was the reality, television show *Naked and Afraid,* which airs on the Discovery Channel. *Naked and Afraid* captures the struggles of two strangers, one man and one woman, who are stranded in a remote and inhospitable location. The goal is to make it through the 21-day challenge relying only on primitive survival skills.

The contestants face extreme adversity ranging from hunger and thirst to hypothermia, sickness, sunburn, and a never-ending battle with insects and other pests. During the challenge, they must pick a suitable area to build shelter, find food and water, and build a fire, while dealing with the psychological and physical effects of starvation and exposure to the elements. And yes, they must do all these things while being completely *naked*.

When my wife first told me about the show, I refused to watch. I thought it was just an excuse for the Discovery Channel to show nudity during prime time. But I am glad I did because the show really drives home the lesson that if you want to be successful, you have to maintain a positive attitude.

Naked and Afraid changed how I think about the old adage "attitude is everything." I watched capable survivalists succumb to negativity and invariably fail. In one show, a female survivalist ended up tapping out on day 19 simply because she was depressed and lonely. However other less experienced survivalists overcame the worst odds and completed the challenge with a positive attitude. Simply put, attitude did matter and in a very big way. It gave the successful contestants that extra edge that kept them going through the worst of times.

After watching a season of *Naked and Afraid* and seeing how much of a role attitude plays in success, my wife and I have chosen to be irrationally positive in the face of adversity, and it makes a noticeable difference in how we approach our problems. Thinking positively about difficult situations has opened the door to ideas that have helped us overcome numerous issues. It will work for your marriage too.

Cheerfulness

As I mentioned in an earlier chapter, I am not naturally cheerful. My natural disposition is a little acerbic, and that can easily degenerate into grumpiness. But that grumpiness almost destroyed my marriage in its first year.

Cheerfulness is especially important for men because being cheerful is a necessary ingredient of being swashbuckling. If you watch any of the old Errol Flynn movies, his hero is always smiling and cheerful, even in the midst of a life-threatening duel. I believe that a swashbuckling nature is one of the things that women want. This is one of the reasons that so many women are attracted to bad boys—men who have a devil may care attitude toward danger. Being cheerful is a way of becoming swashbuckling in daily life.

Even if your marriage is currently experiencing some difficulties, adopting a cheerful disposition can start repairing any damage that has been done. Like anything of value, it is not a "quick fix." Don't wake up cheerful for one day or even for a month and expect your spouse to praise you. Rather, think of every day that you are cheerful as writing a deposit to your spouse's emotional bank account.

As with a positive attitude, being cheerful will not just benefit your marriage, but every area of your life. It will be especially helpful in providing your children with a model of how a healthy adult should act.

Gratitude and Appreciation

One of the laws of the universe is that if you do not appreciate something, you will lose it. If you don't appreciate something, you tend to ignore it or even denigrate it. This applies to people as well as things.

In all the failed marriages that I have seen, the spouses started to take each other for granted long before the relationship went south. In each case, the husband and wife blew their spouses negative characteristics out of proportion while they minimized their good qualities.

How do you appreciate your husband or wife? It starts with attitude—a resolution that you will appreciate your spouse regardless of his or her flaws.

It also helps if you pray for your spouse and thank God for the gift of your spouse. Even if you do not "feel" gratitude and appreciation at that moment, merely saying the words will help actualize those sentiments.

Finally, show your spouse that you appreciate him or her by your actions. Occasionally, let your wife sleep in or make your husband breakfast in bed. Telling your spouse that you appreciate him or her is good too, but not nearly as effective as action.

Persistence and Fortitude

I have some Mormon friends so I've been invited to a lot of events that were primarily for Mormons. One of the things that surprised me is that many young Mormons have had brief marriages that ended in divorce. The reason it is surprising is that the Church of Jesus Christ of Latter-day Saints has a fairly high understanding of marriage. In Mormon theology, marriage is supposed to be virtually indissoluble. Why, then, are so many young Mormons getting divorced?

I believe the reason is poorly set expectations. Many young Mormons are very innocent by modern day standards. They are taught about all the wonderful aspects of marriage such as love, romance, companionship, and sex, but they are not sufficiently informed about the difficulties that couples will encounter. Their innocence combined with romantic notions often leads them to make bad choices when selecting a spouse. And when they encounter struggles in their marriage, it makes them less able to cope.

Marriage *is* about love, romance, companionship, and sex. But it is also about raising children, working 50 hours a week, washing dishes, doing laundry, and replacing a leaky faucet. It's about caring for your spouse when they are sick. It's about seeing them in the morning before they've showered or put on make up. It's about growing old together. In other words, marriage, like life, is a marathon, not a sprint. And it can get grueling at times.

To develop persistence and fortitude, embrace all the struggles as well as the romance and companionship. It is okay to try to minimize unpleasant experiences, but when they come, meet them with joy. When we look, we will find that the challenges we faced will become part of the cherished memories of our lives together.

Forgiveness

It is impossible to live together as a family without forgiveness. There is some truth to the phrase, "forgive and forget." While it might not be possible to truly forget transgressions that our spouse may have committed, we have to live as if we have forgotten it. When we forgive someone, we are wholly reconciled with that person.

True forgiveness means that a mistake your spouse made last year does not resurface in an argument that you have today. It also means that you release any desire to exact revenge upon your spouse for something that he or she has done.

If you choose to harbor an unwillingness to forgive your spouse, it will eventually develop into resentment. You will resent your spouse for what she did, and she will resent you for not forgiving her. Once resentment gets into a person's heart, it is very difficult to remove, and it could result in the death of the marriage.

While we are on the topic of forgiveness, it would be worthwhile mentioning what might be the most hurtful transgression when it comes to marriage—infidelity.

If, God forbid, infidelity should occur in your marriage, it is serious enough that you should not try to handle it all by yourself. If there is ever a cause for marriage counseling, this is it. Seek out a wise, godly, and knowledgeable pastor or counselor to help you discern how to handle the situation.

A Sense of Adventure

A final attitude to adopt for a successful marriage is a sense of your marriage as being an adventure. Richard Branson, the founder of the Virgin Group, said, "if happiness is the goal—and it should be—then adventure should be a top priority." I agree.

In a way, marriage is like the journey undertaken by Bilbo Baggins in J.R.R. Tolkien's wonderful novel, *The Hobbit*. Before he is recruited for his journey, Bilbo is very happy living in his quiet hobbit hole. At first he is reticent to go on the journey because it takes him far away from everything that he has ever known and it exposes him to dangers he never dreamed of. But as his journey progresses, Bilbo is changed into a different person. After Bilbo's adventure is over, he realizes that it was the defining moment of his life.

Marriage is like that. We have no idea what we will encounter on this path. Certainly, there will be joys and sadness, plenty of fun, and perhaps even some danger. In the end, we will be forever changed by this marvelous adventure called marriage.

Here are the steps to make all of these attitudes active in your life and in your marriage.

1. **Commit:** Make a firm decision that you will live with these attitudes no matter what the circumstances are. You can make this decision for yourself even if your spouse is not willing to commit. Your attitude cannot help but affect your spouse over time.

2. **Reinforce:** If you simply make the commitment to live with these attitudes but never review them, you will eventually drop them from your life. The best way is to read a short statement every morning before starting your day. You can write your own or you can use the following statement:

   "I will live this day with a sense of adventure. I will be positive and cheerful. I will push through every obstacle and not give in to discouragement. I am thankful for my (husband or wife) and for my children."

3. **Review:** Every evening before you go to bed, do a quick (less than five minutes) checkpoint of how you did at living out these attitudes during the day. Benjamin Franklin used a literal checklist for this purpose. I prefer to use questions:

   - Did I hold a relentlessly positive attitude today?
   - Was I cheerful to my spouse, my children, and my co-workers?
   - Do I appreciate my spouse? Did I do anything to show my appreciation today?
   - Did I work through the difficulties of this day with fortitude? Or did I let obstacles deter my progress?
   - Was I forgiving toward my spouse today?
   - Did I live this day with a joyful sense of adventure?

4. **Enlist your spouse:** Ask your spouse to commit to living life with these attitudes by applying steps 1 through 3. No one is perfect and there will inevitably be situations when your circumstances will bring you down. If you slip into negativity, your spouse can lift you back up. If both of you are living in this manner, your results will be much better.

5. **Meditate:** Meditate on the following bible verses. They are reminders that these attitudes are not unrealistic. Rather, they are attitudes that we are exhorted to cultivate.

   - **Being Positive:** "If God be for us, who can be against us?" (Romans 8:31)

   - **Cheerfulness:** "A merry heart maketh a cheerful countenance: but by sorrow of the heart the spirit is broken." (Proverbs 15:13)

   - **Gratitude:** "Rejoice evermore. Pray without ceasing. In every thing give thanks: for this is the will of God in Christ Jesus concerning you." (1 Thessalonians 5:16-18)

   - **Fortitude:** "And endurance (fortitude) develops maturity of character." (Romans 5:4)

   - **Was I forgiving toward my spouse today?** "Love... keeps no record of wrongs." (1 Corinthians 13:4-5)

   - **Did I live this day with a joyful sense of adventure?** "And whatsoever ye do, do it heartily, as to the Lord, and not unto men." (Colossians 3:23)

8. Avoid The Eight Common Communication Mistakes

A book about marriage would not be worth its salt without a chapter on the importance of communication. Communication may be the single most important skill for maintaining a satisfying marriage. But communicating effectively is not as straightforward as it sounds. There are not only many forms of communication—verbal, nonverbal, and written—but there are also helpful and harmful ways of communicating as well.

Lack of communication is one of the most common complaints of couples, but the problem is usually not an absence of communication so much as it is ineffective communication. But why is poor communication so common?

For starters, although we learn lots of things in school, most of us are never taught good communication techniques. We can go through our entire lives without realizing that we could improve our communication skills.

The other reason is that it is easy for poor communication to go undiagnosed. Couples may feel that their partner just "doesn't get it" instead of realizing that the misunderstanding stems from ineffective communication. Fortunately, problems in communicating are not inevitable. Through awareness of the following eight communication mistakes, you and your spouse will be able to dramatically improve the quality of communication in your marriage.

Eight Common Communication Mistakes

Mistake #1: Ephemeral Communication

Too often, couples think they are great communicators simply because they spend a lot of time talking to each other, but in reality they are simply engaging in ephemeral communication. This type of communication is particularly deceptive because it tricks a couple into believing that they are effectively communicating when they aren't really talking about anything significant at all.

Almost everyone is guilty of ephemeral communication. It's a way to talk to your partner while conveniently ignoring the bigger issues in the relationship. It is easier to talk about the news, celebrities, or work banalities instead of tackling difficult issues. This can lead to important issues being left unresolved.

If you are lucky, things will eventually come to a head in an argument. At least that way you have a chance to fix the issue. If you are unlucky, your spouse may remain silent. The source of the problem may remain unspoken allowing it to fester and lead to bitterness or even disgust. By the time you finally learn about it, it may be too late to repair the relationship.

Fixing Ephemeral Communication: Ephemeral communication is really a way of avoiding conflict. The best way to correct it is to set up a weekly time when you can discuss difficult issues. This is called the "Family Business Meeting" but it is really a meeting between the husband and the wife. It should take place once a week at a set time.

Allocate 30 minutes for your Family Business Meeting, but it doesn't have to go that long. A formal agenda is not necessary, but I do know couples that actually go in with a list of things that they'd like to discuss.

The agenda for the Family Business Meeting can be any issue that is affecting your family or marriage. You know going into this meeting that all the big issues are on the table. Here are some ideas of types of things you might raise in this meeting:

- Would you like your husband to show more ambition in increasing his salary?

- Do you think that the family eats out too much and that it would be better to have more home cooked meals?

- Where will the children go to preschool? How will you pay for it?

- What housing repairs need to be made?

- Are you concerned about the amount of time your spouse spends on social media?

- Are you happy with the amount of physical affection in the relationship?

In order for the Family Business Meeting to be successful, the most basic rule is that you have to come at it from the perspective of problem solving, not accusation. Avoiding the other Common Communication Mistakes will help you keep your meetings productive.

Mistake #2: Hurtful Communication

Another common mistake among couples is using hurtful communication. Instead of building each other up, some couples use communication to tear the other person down.

Hurtful communication can take many different forms. It could be rolling your eyes at your partner in response to what they've said, using biting sarcasm, or letting your emotions get the better of you so that you yell at your spouse. While releasing that negative emotion might have felt good at the moment, it could really upset your spouse. Starting a conversation off with anger is a sure fire way to argue and accomplish nothing.

Fixing Hurtful Communication: Remember that timing and approach are everything. When you need to address an issue with your boss you don't charge through the door like an angry bear. You take a moment to gather your wits, have your talking points in hand and proceed in a levelheaded manner.

The same tactics should be employed with your spouse. Get rid of the negativity first, by taking a few deep breaths or even exercising. When your head is clear and your emotions are in check, you can have a rational and effective talk with your spouse.

Another tactic that can help in avoiding hurtful communication is to always use the "assumption of good will." Always put the best possible interpretation on the actions and words of your spouse.

Both of these tactics take awareness and practice, but putting them into effect will make a noticeable difference in your relationship.

Mistake #3: Absolute Statements

Using absolute terms such as "always" or "never" can inhibit effective communication. Here are some examples of bad uses of absolutes:

- "You always leave me alone with the kids."

- "You never put the dishes away."

- "You are always tired."

When "always" and "never" are used in an argument, it is almost guaranteed to get him or her to bristle at the statement because it is usually not true. Even if it is true, these are "fighting words," not words that are designed to solve a problem. Their only purpose is to antagonize the other person.

The use of "always" and "never" is not just referring to the person's behavior, it is also implying that they are insensitive and selfish for "always" or "never" doing a certain thing. If your goal is to have a constructive conversation, leave "always" and "never" out of it.

Another use of absolute statements is a threat to end the marriage. Even in the heat of an argument, saying, "I want a divorce," can put you on the road that leads to divorce court. Using ultimatums such as "change or I will file for divorce" have the same effect.

Fixing Absolute Statements: The fix for this is very easy. Both you and your spouse should resolve to never use "always" and "never" when describing each other's behavior—especially during an argument. Also agree to be held accountable when you do slip into using this type of language.

Instead of absolute statements, use accurate descriptions of the behavior that is bothering you. For example, if you feel that your family eats out too often, don't say to your wife, "you never cook dinner at home." Instead, it would be better to say, "we should try to make dinner at home more often. It would be healthier and it will save us money as well."

Finally, never threaten to end your marriage. Make the word "divorce" a dirty word in your household.

Mistake #4: Character Attacks

Another ineffective form of communication involves attacks on the person's character. These are particularly hurtful because it means that not only are the person's actions bad, the actual person is bad. Here are some examples:

- "You're a weak man," or "You're a wimp."

- "Mother was right when she said I should have married Richard."

- "You're a lousy cook."

- "You are a lousy lay."

- "You're lazy."

These attacks are extremely dangerous for a relationship because they imply that there is something immutably wrong about the person. It provides the recipient with no constructive feedback. There is nothing that he or she can do to change.

And the sting of these attacks does not go away. The person who has been called "weak," "lazy," or who has been told that, "I should have married Richard," will probably not forget the words even after they have been forgiven.

Fixing Character Attacks: An effective communicator can separate the issue from the person. This means targeting problematic behaviors and finding positive solutions for the problem.

This means that you don't attack the person's character or "take cheap shots." So, if a woman thinks that her husband should pursue a particular job promotion, she should tell him that explicitly rather than saying, "you are lazy."

Mistake #5: Passive-Aggressive Communication

Passive-aggressive communication can be quite devastating in a marriage. It occurs when one spouse communicates using sarcasm or jokes that sting but only hint at the problem at hand.

The problem with passive-aggressive communication is that the person dishing out the commentary is never able to accurately express his or her feelings. Conversely, the person on the receiving end is hit with barbs and jabs that will automatically put them on the defensive without letting them know the root of the problem.

Fixing Passive-Aggressive Communication: Scholars who have studied communication tell us that passive-aggressive communication stems from a fear of expression. People who resort to passive-aggressive tactics use it as armor to cover their own insecurities about being unable to express themselves.

If your spouse is using passive-aggressive communication, approach him or her with compassion and caution. Create a safe and trusting environment where he or she can talk freely without judgment. This is difficult because it means that you will have to listen to their criticism without reacting in a negative way.

Once a couple gets into a regular routine of talking honestly and openly with one another, without judgment, then passive-aggressive communication will disappear.

If you are the one who is guilty of using passive-aggressive language, there is another great reason to stop using it—it makes you a miserable person. While I was in college, I developed a very sarcastic attitude toward everything. My friends actually enjoyed it because I made lots of funny comments about other people. But I noticed that it was starting to affect how I viewed the world. My sarcastic attitude colored my perception so that nothing looked good.

Then I ran across this quote by Scottish philosopher Thomas Carlyle: "Sarcasm I now see to be, in general, the language of the devil; for which reason I have long since as good as renounced it." After reading that, I dropped sarcasm entirely from my personal life and my outlook improved as a result.

Mistake #6 Invalidating Feelings

When you invalidate your spouse's feelings, you make the mistake of not acknowledging their positive or negative emotions. Instead you might ignore, belittle, or minimize their feelings. Some examples of invalidating feelings are: "Stop blowing this out of proportion!" or "Your problem is not important. I have bigger fish to fry."

When we were expecting our first child, my wife asked me to help in creating a registry for the baby with items such as the crib, car seat, and stroller. I had no idea about what to look for, so I let my wife's friend, an experienced mom, step in and guide my wife. What I completely failed to understand is how important it was to my wife that I help in the process. It wasn't important to me so I just dismissed my wife's feelings.

It works the other way as well. It's possible to put a damper on someone's positive feelings. Let's say your husband spends the entire weekend painting the house. He will likely be very proud of his work and he will hope that you are pleased as well. But if your only reaction is, "now you have to fix the bathroom," it will make him feel unappreciated.

The problem with invalidating feelings, aside from the obvious hurtful and dismissive nature of the behavior, is that it makes future communication more difficult. When one spouse invalidates their partner's feelings on a regular basis, it increases the odds that their partner will just shut down emotionally. This creates a very destructive barrier in the marriage.

Fixing Invalidating Feelings: Remember that feelings whether right or wrong, are still feelings and everyone is entitled to have them. As a loving husband or wife, it is your responsibility to really listen to your spouse and acknowledge his or her feelings. Try to understand why your spouse feels this way, but even if you cannot understand, never dismiss what you are hearing.

When you validate feelings you build trust and deepen the level of communication. Your spouse will be more willing to share concerns or ideas, which leads to overall better communication.

Mistake #7 Bringing Up the Past

Bringing up past hurts is another common communication mistake. It usually goes something like this: Husband and wife are having a disagreement when things get heated. The wife brings up some hurtful event from the past even though it has only a tangential relation to the disagreement. The husband feels unjustly attacked and tries to counter his wife's accusations about the past hurt. The end result is that the couple ends up arguing about the past rather than addressing the present issue. The argument ends up being a waste of time that leaves both parties unhappy.

Bringing up the past hurts your spouse because he or she can't change the past. It is also a reminder that you have not forgiven or forgotten the past behavior. You are nursing a grudge.

Fixing Bringing Up the Past: Both of you must adopt the rule to never, never, never bring up past wrongs in an argument. This takes discipline. It means that you have to confront the real issue and not use the past as a defense mechanism.

The flip side of the coin is that you must truly forgive past wrongs. This is difficult because we all tend to keep a ledger of past wrongs—unfortunately we are not as good at remembering the good things that have been done for us. Getting rid of the ledger is critical to a happy marriage. You can't "keep score."

If your husband did something insensitive early in your marriage, it is all right to raise the issue with him so that he is aware of how his behavior made your feel. However, once the issue has been aired, let go of it and never bring it up again. Your mantra should be "forgive and forget."

Mistake #8 Hearing Instead of Listening

Simply hearing words is very different from truly listening and understanding the message that is trying to be communicated. Like the other communication mistakes, a failure to listen can lead to big problems in your marriage.

There are many ways this can occur. One way is selective hearing—picking out words and phrases that the listener wants to hear to suit his own agenda. Another way is spending time crafting a rebuttal to an argument rather than paying attention to what your spouse is saying. The last way is simple distraction—focusing on something other than what the person is saying.

The message that not listening sends to your spouse is that he or she isn't very important to you—definitely not the feeling you want to convey if your plan is to stay married.

Fixing Poor Listening Skills: Listening is more than just hearing the words your spouse is saying, it involves really understanding them and the nuances that go along with them, such as tone of voice and body language. A good listener doesn't just listen for key words and bits that will help their case; they listen completely and without judgment.

So how do you become a great listener?

- Don't interrupt the other person. Let them speak before you respond. In some group therapy sessions, a counselor will pass around a talking stick. Only the person holding the stick may speak. If necessary, implement something along these lines to help you stay quiet and focused.

- Eliminate distractions. Turn off the TV, put down your smartphone, and turn off the computer. E-mails, texts, or even unfinished chores can wait. Sit down, make eye contact, and truly attend to your spouse.

- Keep an open mind. Avoid jumping to conclusions and be mindful of emotional responses. Think before you speak.

- Listen intently. Refrain from crafting responses until your spouse has finished stating their case. Instead, pay attention to their tone of voice, gestures, and body language. Listening intently will avoid communication breakdowns and greatly improve your marriage.

Tying It All Together

Communication is a key skill for every successful marriage, but learning good communication skills strikes many people, especially men, as being a bit hokey. I happen to be a little skeptical of soft skills like communication myself.

However, I urge you to suspend judgment and work diligently to avoid each of the eight mistakes listed in this chapter. Return to this chapter often to check how you are doing. I believe you will find that this is one of the most powerful tools in making your marriage better.

9. Avoid Money Traps

Issues surrounding money are frequent sources of conflict in a marriage. Surprisingly, many couples enter marriage without having any conversations about how to handle money. Once they are married, they find out that their partner has a radically different philosophy when it comes to spending and saving. If you are not in sync, it can spell disaster for the marriage.

In this chapter, I will discuss some of the common pitfalls regarding money, and share some tips on how you can avoid them.

Our Capitalist Economy

There are lots of things to criticize about our capitalist society. Most of the complaints come from people who would prefer a socialist model such as that exists in Europe today or even the old Soviet-style socialism. These individuals believe that capitalism inordinately enriches a small group of people while it oppresses the masses. They argue that an economy that was centrally managed, say by a panel of Harvard-trained economists, would do a much better job of distributing resources equally among people.

Despite this criticism, it is plainly apparent that the free market economy has lots of advantages over the socialist model. For example, the old Communist bloc countries had problems feeding their people. These countries found out the hard way that even their brainiest economists could not get bread, meat, and vegetables into the hands of people as good as the free market.

While the free market works better than centrally planned economies, it does create a different set of problems. The biggest being that it creates a culture of consumerism. We are constantly bombarded with messages to buy, buy, buy—often for things that we don't need or which does not tangibly make our lives better.

The vast majority of people join this culture of consumerism without giving it a second thought. For married people, this leads to a frenetic lifestyle where both parents are constantly rushing. It leaves little time to unwind or to enjoy each other as a family.

Being part of the consumerist culture also increases the chances that you will become a "wage slave." A wage slave is a person who cannot leave a job that he hates because it is necessary to fund the consumerist lifestyle. Even though it is not, technically speaking, slavery, it is very similar to slavery because we lack true freedom. Being a wage slave can lead to depression, irritability, and health problems.

Fortunately, there is a movement of people who are "waking up" from living the consumerist lifestyle. They understand that freedom is more valuable than having the latest gadget or the latest German car.

The culture of consumerism is one of the biggest obstacles to successfully staying married. In the following pages, I discuss some potential money traps that have been created by our culture, and how to escape them.

Overspending by One Spouse

Probably the most common trap is that one spouse spends too much while the other is more frugal with money.

I had a coworker named Jim who found out after he got married that his new wife, Caitlin, had a spending problem. She came to the marriage with over $20,000 in credit card debt that she was only paying the minimum monthly payments for. But that wasn't the worst of it. She also couldn't control herself when it came to buying new things. One day Jim came home to learn that she had just bought new curtains for all the windows in the house even though they had just finished replacing the curtains a few months before. Caitlin was adding credit card debt faster than he could pay it down.

Up until that point, Jim had been a very passive man. He hadn't even initially pursued Caitlin. She was the one who asked him out on their first date. She led during their entire courtship. She was even the one who planned when and where Jim would "pop the question." If one were forced to put a label on Jim, the best label would be that he was a classical "beta male." He always let someone else run the show.

But when he realized what was happening, Jim transformed and took charge. He tapped into leadership reserves that even he did not know were buried within him. First, he sat down with his wife to try to understand what was happening. To his credit, he understood that Caitlin was not deliberately trying to sabotage their finances. Rather, she was buying out of an emotional need. This realization allowed Jim to approach the problem *working with his wife* as part of their joint mission. It wasn't as a domineering father disciplining a disobedient child.

Jim approached the problem by discussing what their mutual vision was for their family. How many children did they want to have? What type of home did they want to purchase? What type of vacations did they want to take? By looking at the problem from the perspective of the joint mission, Jim was able to get Caitlyn to buy into the plan for getting their finances back on track.

His next step was to shut down the overcharged credit card accounts. Taking this step prevented his wife from adding anything more to the debt. While this step doesn't solve the problem by itself, it does stop the problem from becoming any greater.

Jim also took complete control of the couple's finances. He paid the bills, monitored the checking, savings, and investment accounts. He instituted a rule that he would have to approve all purchases over $100. This enabled Caitlyn to continue to buy necessities like groceries, but minimized the risk of large purchases that would break the bank.

You may be thinking that these were draconian restrictions that would upset his wife. Interestingly, Jim's wife wholeheartedly agreed to the new limitations and she loved the new "alpha male" leadership characteristics that Jim had displayed. Now that she had a mission to fulfill with her husband, she didn't see this as a punishment, but as a way that she could contribute to making their family successful.

Jim and Caitlin's final step was to draw up a budget. They were both working, so their cash flow was good. The budget wasn't too Spartan. It allowed reasonable additions to their wardrobes, allowances for a weekly meal in a restaurant, and other entertainment spending. By keeping some discretionary spending in the budget, they were able to continue to enjoy life while gradually paying down the outstanding credit card debt.

The story ends happily as Jim and Caitlin were able to pay down their debt over the course of several years. They had three children and were eventually able to purchase their dream home. Twelve years later, they are still together after having weathered a storm that would have wiped out other couples.

In summary, if one partner in the relationship has a problem with spending, take the following steps to resolve the problem:

1. Don't assume that spouse is deliberately trying to hurt the marriage. Rather, approach your spouse as a partner in your joint mission. Taking this approach will allow you to tackle the problem without assigning blame.
2. Close or restrict access to credit cards with existing debt. This will staunch the bleeding.
3. Develop a monthly spending budget and stick to it. Make sure that there is some discretionary spending for dining and entertainment.

Keeping Up With The Joneses

The consumerist culture that we all live in might be inducing both spouses into overspending in an effort to fit in with their neighbors, friends, or coworkers. This is keeping up with the Joneses and it is a money trap that can prevent you from ever experiencing financial freedom.

Unless you are like the American Transcendentalist author Henry David Thoreau who spent two years living in a cabin on the shores of Walden Pond, you are likely influenced at least slightly by what your neighbors are doing.

I wouldn't call my neighborhood affluent, but I can definitely see keeping up with the Joneses at work. At first I noticed that one neighbor had purchased a new Mercedes-Benz C class car. A couple of months later, the neighbor across the street from the first neighbor bought the same car. As I walked through the neighborhood this afternoon I noticed that yet a third neighbor in that section has bought the exact same car. I am not sure where the trend will stop. Perhaps the entire street will gradually become Mercedes-Benz C class owners.

It is possible that all of my neighbors have come to agree that the Mercedes-Benz provides an exceptional value for an automobile. But more likely, they are just keeping up with the Joneses.

At other times, the pressure comes not from our own neighbors but from what we see on television. For instance, the reality show called *Keeping Up With Kardashians*, subjects its viewers to lots of beautiful scenery. The Kardashians live in gigantic, opulent homes. They drive expensive cars, dress in designer clothes, and they vacation in exotic locations.

If you manage to avoid watching mind-numbing reality television shows, the scripted series are no better. The Fox series *Empire* is about hip-hop moguls who are not known for their low-key lifestyles. Even the popular HBO series *Game of Thrones* is mostly about the lives of the rich and famous even though it takes place in a medieval fantasy world. It is easy to feel a let down when your get into your five year old Honda.

The key to resisting the demands of the consumerist culture is to recognize it for what it is. The advertisers have honed their profession to a science. They know precisely how to induce us to buy. As powerful as these messages are, they cannot trump our free will. We can always swim against the tide.

Once again, having a clear family mission is the key to resisting the demands of the consumerist culture. Part of our family mission is that we want our children to be raised by family, not by day care. My wife and I both had working moms. Our live-in grandmothers raised us while our mothers were away. We don't have the option of a similar arrangement so we decided that my wife would stay home after she gave birth to our first child.

The decision to only have one income has limited us in some ways. We don't take the lavish vacations we see some of our friends take. Although our cars are in good working condition, they are not the shiny, high-end models that our neighbors drive. But it also has some benefits. My wife is less harried than she'd be if she had to work, which means that I am less harried as well. And we hope that the individual attention is good for our children's development. Focusing on the benefits of our family mission makes it much easier to say 'no' to keeping up with the Joneses.

After you have established your family mission, the next step is to identify the areas where you spend the most. Examine your monthly spending to see where the weak points are. For the time being leave off the necessary expenses like mortgage or rent, groceries, and utilities. For a first pass, focus on discretionary spending:

- **Cable:** Cable television and internet can represent a giant monthly bill so it deserves close scrutiny. There are many ways to reduce this bill. One option is to investigate switching to one of the streaming services that are available such as Amazon Fire TV, Apple TV, or Netflix. Another option is to investigate switching service providers. To entice new customers to switch, these providers frequently offer low priced contracts that can save you nearly $1000 per year.

- **Restaurants:** Eating out is an expensive affair especially after you include the tip, parking fees, gas burned to get there, and your time—and often the food is not nearly as good as what you can make at home. Also, don't overlook less obvious expenses like that daily, overpriced cappuccino.

- **Movies, video games, or books:** My personal weakness is books. I am a voracious reader and a lifelong bibliophile. The only way to curb this is to set limits of how many books, movies, or video games you will purchase or rent during the month.

- **Clothing or accessories:** Looking your best is important, but it is possible to do without breaking the bank. Avoid purchasing clothing or accessories, such as purses or shoes, out of an emotional need.

- **Toys:** We love our children so the temptation is to get them everything, but having fewer toys does not necessarily mean a lower quality of childhood. Sometimes the best toys are the simplest ones because they require imagination to use.

- **Cars:** One of the primary ways of keeping up with the Joneses is by making sure we have cars that match or exceed the cars owned by our neighbors and friends. But keeping up with the Joneses in this regard can be one of the most dangerous things that you can do to your family's long-term financial stability. I cover this in more detail a little later in this chapter when I discuss how to deal with debt.

After determining which areas are causing you the most trouble, develop a reasonable monthly budget for each area and stick to it. You can repeat the same exercise with the necessary expenses, but it is usually harder to trim fat from those areas.

Sticking to your monthly budget and remembering your family mission are the best ways of avoiding the trap of keeping up with the Joneses.

Financial Problems Stemming From Addiction

Sometimes, financial problems are the result of one of the spouses having an addiction. This could be a drug or alcohol problem, but it could also be an addiction to something like gambling or pornography. Although some individuals have the will power to simply stop engaging in their addiction without outside help, an addiction will usually require some type of counseling.

I witnessed the damage that addiction can afflict on a family's financial well-being when I was a boy. While I was growing up, my mother had a close friend named Jan that she had met at work. Jan had a son the same age as me so we were natural playmates whenever our mothers got together.

I was just a kid, but I noticed that Jan's family had a different lifestyle than my family did. Whereas we lived in a modest but pleasant suburban home, Jan and her family lived in the inner city in a cramped older house with a tiny lot. Jan's husband Mark supposedly had a high paying union job, but it was clear that the family was not doing well financially.

When I got a little older, my mother told me that the family was struggling because the husband, Mark, had a serious gambling problem. Not only did he spend every penny he earned—he also borrowed to finance his vice.

Because of the distance, my mom and Jan drifted apart. Years later, I learned that Mark had died suddenly while he was still a young man leaving his wife to care for two teenage children.

About 15 years after Mark's death, Jan contacted my mother again. Her life had changed completely after the death of her husband. She moved out of the inner city and purchased a large house in an affluent neighborhood. She also takes frequent trips to Europe—something that she never could have afforded while Mark was alive.

Of course, part of Jan's financial transformation may be attributed to receiving a payout from Mark's life insurance policy, but the larger portion of her success is because she has continued to work and spend within her means. Without the extra burden of having to fund a gambling addiction, she is able to live very well.

Regardless of Jan's ultimate financial success, the sad part of this story is that instead of being the protector of his family, Mark was a destroyer of his family's wealth. It seems cruel to say it, but Mark's family was better off, at least financially, after he was gone. I doubt that any husband or wife would want that to be their legacy.

One of the most hurtful aspects of addiction is that the addict may engage in dishonest behavior to cover up his addiction. A spouse will be able to handle the difficulties involved in overcoming the addiction itself, but he or she may find the lying and obfuscation very disheartening. That is why the addicted partner should be completely open and honest with his or her spouse, even though it will be painful.

Also, addiction is a problem that usually can't be solved by the couple alone. Addicts will often claim that they can control their problem without the need to resort to professional help. Sometimes they can, but it is prudent to err on the side of getting help.

In summary: If you have an addiction, don't hesitate: confess your problem to your spouse and enlist his or her help in conquering the addiction; and don't be ashamed of seeking professional counseling in getting rid of the addiction. Although there is a cult of "rugged individualism" in our culture, the truth is that we can't live without leaning on others. Get the help you need.

If you find out that your spouse has an addiction, confront him or her but do it in a loving way, assuring him or her of your full support. Strongly suggest that he or she seek professional help. It will also be helpful for you to receive counseling as well so that you know the best way of dealing with your spouse.

Debt

One of the most insidious aspects of our consumer culture is the availability of easy credit. It lulls us into the belief that we can live a lifestyle that we cannot really afford. In other words, it allows us to have champagne taste on a beer budget. It can easily put a couple on a hamster wheel where both husband and wife are working but are unable to get ahead because they are paying high interest on their credit cards, school loans, auto loans, and mortgage.

One approach to avoiding the debt trap is to adopt a debt-free lifestyle. This is the path followed by Jim Bob and Michelle Duggar of the TLC reality television show *19 Kids and Counting*. The Duggars were living a debt-free lifestyle long before they got their television show. They chose to live debt-free early in their marriage after attending a "Financial Freedom Seminar" by Jim Sammons.

For the Duggars, living debt free meant that they were not able to play "keeping up with the Joneses" by accumulating status symbols like expensive cars and designer clothes. Instead, they shopped at thrift stores and followed the motto "Buy used and save the difference." They allocated only $100 a month to entertainment expenses so they didn't have cable television. They even cut their own hair to save on trips to the salon.

The Duggars frugal lifestyle paid off. Within seven years the couple was completely debt free. Being debt free enabled them to pursue other business opportunities that would have been closed off if they were carrying a large debt load.

With any new business venture, there is always a period of time where the business is in a "cash burn" status—it is losing more money than it is making. If a couple has the funds, they can sustain this initial capital outlay.

Most couples can't handle the initial cash burn for long. They are so heavily saddled with debt that they quickly need to reconnect to a corporate job as employees. Thus, many promising businesses end up dying before they are able to reach full profitability.

Freedom from debt enabled Jim Bob to quit working as an employee and become an entrepreneur. He started several successful businesses in addition to purchasing commercial real estate that provides continuous income. Thus, the Duggars were already millionaires before they ever signed up for their TLC television show.

While the Duggar debt-free approach works, it is definitely an austere approach. It also makes it nearly impossible to live in one of the higher cost of living areas such as Los Angeles or New York. Here are six actions that you can take to reduce debt while still allowing your family to enjoy a high quality of life.

A. Don't Use Your Credit Cards to Carry Debt

It is a good idea to carry zero debt on your credit cards even when you have to make large purchases, such as appliances. The interest rates on credit card debt are notoriously high in comparison to other types of loans so try to avoid it like plague. No one should have to go into debt to buy a dress or a suit. If that is the case, it is time to look for a different suit to purchase.

However, credit cards are still useful as a convenient form of payment. As long as you are diligent about paying off your statement in full every month, it makes sense to carry a credit card or two. They are easier to carry than cash and they are more secure than debit cards.

Look for credit cards that you can obtain for no annual fee. Also, look for cards that offer some sort of rewards or points. These can add up surprisingly quickly if you use the card to pay for everyday expenses such as gas and groceries.

Finally, if you have lots of credit card debt, consider taking out a lower interest loan, and paying off your high interest credit cards. By consolidating your debt in this way, you simplify the payment and lower the total interest that you would have to pay.

B. Avoid School Loan Debt

By the time you read this, it is probably too late. You may already be saddled with school loan debt. However, this information may still be helpful to you if you are considering going to college or if you have children who will soon go to college.

Origin of the School Loan Debacle

The widespread availability of student loans is a scam that has been perpetrated by colleges working with the federal government. This started in the 1970s. Colleges and universities had expanded their faculties, staffs, and infrastructure to meet projected demand from the baby boom generation. When the flow of new students began to ebb, the universities lobbied Congress to provide incentives to people to enroll. Congress responded by increasing federally funded student aid and student loans.

Congress' plan worked. Lots of new students flocked to universities. However, colleges responded to the new abundance by increasing tuition rates. College tuition has risen much faster than the income of families. University of Tennessee law professor Glen Harlan Reynolds, who has written extensively on rising education costs, gives some perspective:

> [T]uition for all universities, public and private, increased from 1978 to 2011 at an annual rate of 7.45%. By comparison, health-care costs increased by only 5.8%, and housing, notwithstanding the bubble, increased at 4.3%. Family incomes, on the other hand, barely kept up with the consumer-price index, which grew at an annual rate of 3.8%.

What did universities do with the extra money they were making from the student loan funded gravy train? According to Reynolds, they used "the proceeds to build palatial buildings, reduce faculty teaching loads and, most notably, hire armies of administrators."

While taking out a student loan may make sense if you are attending Harvard or going to medical school, legions of graduates have found that their salaries are much lower than anticipated, leaving them with years of student loans to pay off. This situation can't go on forever. Reynolds goes so far as to call the current situation a "higher education bubble." Eventually, the bubble will burst and educational institutions will face a reckoning, but that doesn't help people who already have student loan debt.

How to Avoid School Loan Debt

The best remedy is to avoid student loans in the first place. The traditional way of doing this is to work, at least part time, while attending college. Using this approach may mean that it takes a little bit longer to complete the degree, but it has the advantage of minimizing or eliminating the need for student loans.

Another way that has opened up in the past few years involves more online learning. This started with independent providers such as Khan Academy, but now even prestigious universities, such as the Georgia Institute of Technology, are starting to make available online degrees. Obtaining an online degree from a reputable school is much more cost effective than an on-campus degree, and while you might miss out on the experience of college parties, you'll be glad that you have no debt when you graduate.

Finally, a third option is to re-think whether you even need to go to college. While I was growing up, it was just assumed that my path would include going to college. In one way, college opens lots of opportunities because it can teach a marketable skill, at least if you avoid the more trendy majors such as feminist studies.

But, a college degree also tends to shrink your horizons as well. The typical liberal arts curriculum teaches students nothing about being an entrepreneur. But even if you get a degree in science, engineering, or math, you will be better suited to becoming an employee than starting your own business. After I graduated, I naturally started looking for a job as an employee rather than thinking about starting my own company. Meanwhile, some of my high school classmates used those four years learning a trade that they later turned into successful businesses.

Our economy is changing. The old employer-employee model is slowly dying. If you have the aptitude, I still would recommend that you go to college, but be careful to select a marketable course of study and select a reasonably priced program. Even then, go into it with an entrepreneurial mindset knowing that there may be fewer jobs available when you graduate.

If you already happen to have student loan debt, the only good news is that the loans tend to be lower interest, so while it may be annoying, you are probably not wasting tons of money to service the interest.

In summary, the best course is to avoid student loan debt, as there does not seem to be any easy way of discharging it once you have it.

C. Don't Always Carry Car Loan Debt

Another common debt trap is to constantly carry car loan debt. This is usually done in the form of a lease. Many couples today never actually own a vehicle. They simply lease one car after another.

There is no question that leasing carries lots of advantages. A new car is usually safer than an older car. Because all the parts are less than two or three years old, they will behave more reliably. Newer cars also spend less time in the shop and they are less costly to maintain than an older car. And we can't deny that the new car smell and feel is a pleasant experience.

But leasing comes with disadvantages as well. The biggest of these is that it requires you to pay a large monthly payment without gaining any equity in the vehicle. If instead, you purchase your car rather than lease, you can plan on significant savings if you keep your car after you have completed your loan payments.

For example, if you buy a car using a four-year loan and keep the car for three years after you have paid off your loan, you would save approximately $12,600 (assuming a monthly payment of $350). The actual savings would be something less than that number because there are still maintenance costs, but the savings are not insubstantial. If you and your wife both have a car, the savings really skyrocket.

On top of your savings for the years while you are not paying for a car loan or a lease, you will have at least some trade in value for your old car when you go to buy a new one. If you have taken care of your old car, this could amount to several thousand dollars even if there is something majorly wrong with the vehicle.

Another way of reducing your car loan debt is to save money up front when you buy your vehicle. Avoid the temptation to buy a flashy car. Go with a cheaper model instead. This is really difficult in our consumer culture. One of our friends recently bought an entry level Porsche even though her three children will literally have to live on peanut butter and jelly for several months to be able to afford it. Her reasoning is that she has been frugal for many years and that she is ready to "live life."

The second way to save up front is to buy a slightly used car. By slightly used, I mean a car that was either used by the dealer as a loaner or a car that has been leased for a year. The fact that a car is slightly used takes thousands of dollars off the price, but doesn't significantly diminish the operating value of the car.

In summary, here is how to reduce your car loan debt:

1. Purchase your cars. Avoid leasing.
2. Buy a high quality vehicle, but don't go top of the line.
3. Try to pay off your car in less than five years.
4. Buy slightly used.

D. Minimize Mortgage Debt and Steer Clear of Aggressive Loans

If there is one debt that is acceptable to carry, it is the mortgage debt associated with the loan on your house.

Mortgage loans are typically at a lower interest rate than other debt, such as credit card debt. Also, property has historically increased in value or at least held steady. This makes a mortgage for a house different than a loan for a car, because most cars decline in value. Finally, the US federal government currently encourages mortgage debt because the interest is tax deductible.

All these factors make a mortgage attractive when compared with other types of debt.

However, there are some caveats. While housing prices tend to go up, there are certain cases when they also go down, sometimes very quickly. I've seen people buy and then lose $200,000 of the value of their home in the space of a few short months. Sometimes the market comes back, and sometimes it does not. Most properties still have not recovered their value after the 2007 housing bubble crisis. There are also continued calls for the government to do away with the mortgage interest tax deduction because it favors the middle and upper classes. So while it is usually a good bet to take out a mortgage on a property, it is far from a sure bet.

There are a few money traps associated with mortgages that you need to be aware of.

- **Adjustable Rate Mortgages (ARMs).** The ARM is a mechanism used by lenders to enable you to buy a more expensive house than what your current means allow. An ARM loan means that the interest rate can fluctuate a certain percentage each year based on some interest rate indicator, such as the prime-lending rate. Sometimes, an ARM can work in your favor and the interest rate will go down, but it can just as easily go up. If rates go up, this can leave you with a prohibitively high mortgage rate.

- **Balloon Payments.** A balloon payment on a mortgage allows a lender to provide you with a lower interest rate up front, but specifies that a large payment be paid several years out. Practically speaking, the person buying the mortgage will need another mortgage loan to pay off the balloon payment. This might not be such a bad idea if the interest rates are lower when the balloon payment is due, but it could be a disaster if the interest rates increase in the interim.

- **Too Big of a Mortgage.** The conventional wisdom has been to get the most house that you can afford. The reasoning is that your salary will continue to increase so that even if your mortgage were difficult to pay in the beginning, it would become easier as you earned more. The problem is, wage and salary growth has been stagnant for at least a decade. In other words, it would be more prudent to buy a house that you can comfortably afford today.

- **Being Too Aggressive with Loan Duration.** I have to confess that I am guilty of this trap. Because I believe in avoiding debt, the loan I got for our house was for 15 years instead of the usual 30-year mortgage. This meant that we had higher monthly payments but that we would pay our house off more quickly. The higher payments were fine as long as both my wife and I were working. However, once we had our first baby, my wife stayed home. This made living on one salary a whole lot harder than it needed to be.

  Instead, I suggest that you go for a 30-year mortgage, and, if you can, pay additional principle each month. You will be able to pay your mortgage down just as quickly but you will have the flexibility of having a lower payment if you need it.

In summary, mortgage debt is still the most acceptable form of debt that you can carry.

- For most couples, the best mortgage will be the traditional 30-year fixed mortgage.
- Avoid buying a house that will make you "house poor" as there is no guarantee that your salary will grow as quickly as you plan.

Consider Combining Your Finances

Another money-related issue is the question of whether or not spouses should combine their finances. Should you share a checking account or should each person maintain his own account? Should you hold title to your house jointly?

There is no right answer here. My wife and I decided to combine everything so that everything is held jointly. I was already financially established but my wife was just starting out so, technically speaking, my wife "gained" a lot in the process of combining our resources. Divorce lawyers might be horrified by what I did, but I never went into marriage thinking that divorce was an option. For us, combining our resources was a sign that we were no longer just separate individuals, but that we were a family.

One disadvantage of the combined finance approach is that it is harder for us to buy each other presents without the other being aware of it since we both have access to all the transactions. We believe this is a small price to pay for the convenience of both of us being able to do everything with our combined resources.

Estate Planning

Holding everything jointly may have one estate planning advantage: if one partner dies, the jointly held property generally transfers to the other spouse automatically without the need for it to pass through probate process.

Probate is the legal process that takes place after a person dies. The purpose of probate is to ensure that all the deceased's creditors and beneficiaries get their due amount. Probate courts try to make the process administration as simple as possible, but it can still take several months to close the estate.

Until everything has been sorted out, the beneficiaries may not be able to access the funds that are part of the deceased's estate. This means that if the husband dies with a large lump of cash in a checking account owned solely by him, his wife may not be able to access it immediately. If, on the other hand, the account were jointly held, it would have passed immediately to his wife.

Of course, the above should not be construed as legal advice. The laws vary from state to state, and everyone's situation is different, so be sure to talk with a qualified local attorney prior to making any estate planning decisions.

By the way, I strongly advise that all married couples have wills written. This applies even if you currently do not own a lot of assets. It is just a way to ensure that your spouse and your children are taken care of in the manner that you desire. Because there are so many things to consider, I don't recommend that you use a "do it yourself" service. Find a qualified local lawyer to draft the wills.

Keeping Resources Separate

While we combined our finances, we also know successful couples that have kept everything separate. There may be several reasons for doing this.

In the old days, couples got married younger when they were just starting out. It made sense for couples to hold everything in common. Nowadays, people tend to get married later after they already become financially established. They've established their own spending habits. In this case, the husband and wife may prefer the freedom of separate accounts.

Some couples adopt a hybrid approach where joint expenses, such as mortgage payments and utility expenses, get paid out of a joint account, but each person still maintains his or her separate account.

In summary, combining your finances has some benefits, but it may not be right for every couple. The key to any of these approaches is that both of you are in full agreement with the approach.

Adopt The Virtue of Simplicity

"Don't create needs for yourself." –Josemaria Escriva

A final weapon in our war to prevent money problems from dividing our marriages is the virtue of simplicity.

In its most basic form, simplicity means that we forego collecting more stuff, because it makes our lives harder. When I was growing up, the big status symbol in my neighborhood was having a swimming pool—the bigger the better. Built in pools were more highly coveted over the temporary above ground pools.

Swimming pools are great fun for the kids, but they introduce a lot of unnecessary complexity into your life. If you have a pool, you have to maintain it regularly by adding chlorine, changing the filter, and screening out any big things that may fall into it. You have to drain it before winter comes or keep it heated. There are also lots of pool parts such as the filter or the heater that may break and need to be repaired. If you have a large pool, it may just be less time consuming to hire a pool service that maintains the pool for you, but this costs extra money. Having a pool also exposes you to liability. Pool owners have to be careful to ensure that no children can slip into the pool unattended. In other words, something that is supposed to be fun for the family can quickly become a source of major irritation in your life.

A better approach is to adopt simplicity as a lifestyle. Make your life as uncomplicated as possible. While some people may view simplicity as a form of restriction, it is actually a source of power. Simplicity allows you to live on less so that you have less to fear from losing your job. It frees your time to pursue greater things.

Tying It All Together

Financial problems are one of the biggest stressors on a marriage. By avoiding the most common money traps and adopting the virtue of simplicity you will avoid financial stress and set your marriage on a firm economic foundation.

10. Faith

Do you need to have faith in a supernatural being in order to have a successful marriage? Absolutely not, but if you do, it can be a powerful aid to staying married in difficult times.

If you happen to be an unbeliever, feel free to skip this chapter. But if you do believe, I will discuss how to make your faith operative in your marriage.

There are lots of examples of successful marriages where neither the husband nor the wife had faith. I know a man who immigrated to the United States from the Peoples' Republic of China. He and his wife have been married for over 30 years. Being raised under the rule of Chairman Mao, they are both atheists, but this has not stopped them from having a successful marriage. At one point, the Chinese government forced the husband to work in Africa for several years while his wife stayed in China. Despite the hardship of being separated for several years, he and his wife remained faithful to each other. They were able to do this because of their strong morals even though they lacked faith.

While faith isn't necessary for a healthy marriage, it can be very helpful. Data compiled by the Georgetown University Center for Applied Research in the Apostolate indicate that the divorce rate is 28% for Catholics, which is high, but it compares favorably with the 40% divorce rate for those with no religious affiliation. The divorce rate for Protestants came in high at 39%, but I suspect there is a good explanation for this phenomenon that I will explain below.

For faith to be a source of strength in a marriage, a superficial faith is not going to cut it. The type of faith that is required to make a strong marriage has to be deep. To be effective, the faith of both husband and wife needs to be active.

Active Faith

The United States is a nominally Christian country. People identify as Catholic, Protestant, or Orthodox, but their actual practice of their faith is often nominal at best. This shallow spirituality will be of almost no value in keeping a marriage together in difficult times. Only a living, active faith can do that. But what does it mean to have an active faith?

I happen to be a Catholic Christian, so I will answer this question from a Catholic perspective, but I think that any sort of Christian can easily apply whatever I say.

Making a profession of faith at some point in the past, say at your baptism, is a good thing, but simply believing at some point in the past isn't enough to make your faith operative. In order to do that, you have to live it. You have to practice it.

If you think about it, faith is really a relationship—a relationship with God. If you had a friend who you only talked to once or twice a year, you probably would not consider them your best friend. Moreover, you probably don't think about the friend you only talk to once or twice a year. They are far from your mind most of the time.

It is no different with your relationship with God. If you only pray once in a while, or if you only go to church on Christmas day, your relationship with him is going to be weak. God will not be at the forefront of your mind.

My wife and I are friends with a Catholic couple who are currently having some problems in their marriage. Apparently, there has been some lack of communication in the marriage and the couple has allowed some resentment to build. Another man started flirting with the wife, and although she has not done anything yet, she has confessed to my wife that she has been responding to the flirting. When my wife challenged her, our friend cut off communication.

Our friends are far from bad people. They are high achievers at work and they are fantastic parents to their children. How then could what appears to be a solid marriage run into trouble?

Although it is impossible for me to know for certain, I do know that this couple doesn't practice their faith. Like most parents, they are extremely busy between work and shuttling their kids to music lessons, soccer practice, and swimming classes. But this busy-ness has a price: they've stopped practicing their faith so that they can fit in all the other activities. They rarely attend Sunday Mass.

I wonder if our friends would be in the same position if they actually lived their faith in close connection to God. My guess would be that they would be less inclined to toy with such a destructive option as infidelity if God played more of a role in their lives.

Here are some steps that you can take to ensure that you are living out your faith:

Attend Weekly Worship

The first step in practicing your faith is to go to church every Sunday. Unfortunately, in our frenetic age, weekly worship is one of the first things that we jettison. It is not a new problem. Even the author of the letter to the Hebrews exhorted the first generation of Christians to "not neglect meeting together, as is the habit of some."

Weekly worship serves two purposes. The primary purpose is the privilege of worshipping God. I say it is a privilege because most people treat going to church as if they were doing God a favor. In reality, it is an honor that God has invited us. Worship is the most important reason for going to church on Sunday.

The secondary purpose of going to church on Sunday is to meet with other believers. It really helps our walk with Christ to know other believers who are also following Him. Friends in the faith can boost our morale when we are flagging and they can bring our failings to our attention if we go astray. Fellow Christians are also part of your tribe—something that we will increasingly need as our society continues to decline.

While meeting with other believers is an important secondary reason for going to church every week, it should never be the only reason for going. I am sure that you know people who go to church solely for the social aspects. They might be heavily involved in doing charitable activities, but there is no vertical dimension to their faith. They merely enjoy the company of other church members.

One final point: *It is imperative to attend church together as a family.* I've seen parents drop their children off for Mass by themselves. Or sometimes the parents will sit in back playing with their smartphone while their kids listen to the sermon. I doubt anyone derives any benefit from treating God in that manner. Whenever possible, husband and wife should attend church and participate together.

Going to church every Sunday is not a guarantee of a virtuous life or a stable marriage, but you can think of it as a lifeline. As long as you are going to church regularly, you are still keeping the door open for God in your life. Therefore, go to church weekly even if you feel hypocritical in doing so.

Have a Deep Prayer Life

A deep prayer life is the single biggest factor in your spiritual health. If you want a profound relationship with God, you have to spend time with him every day. The most important component of a deep prayer life is mental prayer.

What is mental prayer? It is merely spending time talking to God. Formal, memorized prayers can be used to open and close your prayer time, but for the prayer time itself, just use your own words. You don't have to speak aloud.

Try to go in without props. You may wish to read a bible passage or something from a devotional book to stimulate your thoughts, but don't read through your entire meditation.

There is no technique for Christian mental prayer. Different spiritual writers, such as St. Francis de Sales, have proposed a structure to mental prayer. Personally, I have found that I end up thinking about the structure too much rather than just being with the Lord. The method I use is that I just talk to God like I would talk to any other person.

How long should your period of mental prayer be? 15 minutes daily is a minimum for most people.

If you adopt the habit of daily mental prayer, it will quickly become the linchpin of your life. I'll close this section with a few quotes on prayer from a modern day master of the spiritual life, St. Josemaría Escrivá:

You seek the company of friends who, with their conversation and affection, with their friendship, make the exile of this world more bearable for you. There is nothing wrong with that, although friends sometimes let you down.

But how is it you don't frequent daily with greater intensity the company, the conversation, of the great Friend, who never lets you down?

You say that you don't know how to pray? Put yourself in the presence of God, and once you have said, 'Lord, I don't know how to pray!' rest assured that you have begun to do so. The Way, 90.

Pray Together

In addition to praying individually, husband and wife should also pray together as a family. If you have children, you can include them as well. As Jesus tells us in Matthew 18:20, "For where two or three are gathered in my name, there am I among them."

The best way to do this is to make prayer a part of your family's daily life. Bishop Athanasius Schneider has said, "In order to remain faithful to their vocation the Catholic family must practice especially the daily common prayer."

For Catholics, one of the best ways of doing this is by praying a family rosary. Pope Pius XII told a gathering of newlyweds:

> We beseech you, take it to heart to keep this beautiful tradition of Christian families: the common prayer in the evening. The family gathers at the end of each day to implore the Divine blessings and to honor the Immaculate Virgin through the praises of the Rosary for all who sleep under the same roof... Strive to sanctify this even short moment dedicating it to God in order to praise Him and to present to Him your desires, your needs, your sufferings and your occupations. The center of your home must be the Crucified or the image of the Sacred Heart of Jesus: May Christ reign over your home and gather you around Him every day (Address to Newly Married Couples, 12th February 1941).

Instead of the family rosary, Protestant Christians could spend a few minutes in extemporaneous prayer or simply gather together for a short bible reading. The format does not matter as much as the spirit.

Incorporate Ritual into the Life of Your Family

We all have rituals in our life. Every morning, I make breakfast with my son, eat, and shower before leaving for work. We also have annual rituals. Every Thanksgiving, we make the trek to the home of my parents where we partake of the traditional turkey meal. Our lives are literally filled with these secular rituals.

Some religions are also rich in ritual. Judaism and Islam are very detailed as to how a person lives their life on a day-to-day basis down to the point of even prescribing certain prayers after visiting the bathroom. Christianity has a little bit less in the way of daily ritual: Catholicism and Orthodoxy generally have a little more while Protestantism has a little less daily ritual.

Christians also have annual rituals. We are all familiar with the feasts of Christmas and Easter, but there are also the seasons of Advent and Lent that allow us to live with a different rhythm. Advent takes place during the four Sundays preceding Christmas day. Lent is a six-week season that begins with Ash Wednesday and goes on until Easter Sunday. Advent and Lent are seasons of preparation that ask us to focus on renewing our relationship with the Lord through prayer, fasting, and the giving of alms.

Celebrating Advent as a season of preparation is a great way to keep your family from being sucked into the orgy of consumerism that the secular culture engages in during this period. Some Christians celebrate the four weeks of Advent using an advent wreath. This is a small wreath with four candles that can be placed on the table. Every Sunday, the father can lead the family in prayer and light the number of candles corresponding to the week of Advent.

Observing Lent as a penitential season reminds us that Christians are to remain sober in a dissolute age. It also provides us with an opportunity to conquer any bad habits that we have acquired. Most Christians choose to "give up" something during Lent. I've known people who have successfully given up smoking or who have lost weight during Lent. But most importantly, observing Lent provides us with an opportunity to grow closer to the Lord.

Why are rituals important to your marriage? Because they serve as reminders to make Christ part of our day. Without these reminders, it is easy to get caught up in the rush of life and thus neglect our vertical relationship with God. Rituals also remind us that God is a partner in our marriage.

Finally, rituals distinguish your family from other families. Feeling distinctive is a human need. While none of us want to be considered eccentric, we do want to know that we are special in some way. The religious rituals that our family practices have already enabled me to teach our two year old son that sometimes we do things differently from other families. The recognition that your family is distinctive helps to strengthen the family mission, which in turn keeps husband and wife closer to each other.

Remember Your Vows
Our culture puts little emphasis on vows because the entire thrust of our culture is to absolve the individual of any personal responsibility. In this respect we are very strange, because our ancestors took their vows very seriously.

God takes vows very seriously. Numbers 30:2 states, "If a man vows a vow to the Lord, or swears an oath to bind himself by a pledge, he shall not break his word. He shall do according to all that proceeds out of his mouth." This includes vows that were uttered rashly. We are exhorted to be careful about what we say, but if we make a vow, we are bound to fulfill it.

We need to reclaim the concept of vows, and the best way to start is by honoring our marriage vows. Most people probably do not recall the exact words of their wedding vow, but they do remember the gist. That's good, but it is a salutary practice to periodically review your wedding vows.

Review your vows at least once a month, but you may find it helpful to review them weekly. It only takes a few seconds and it has big benefits.

Tying It All Together—A Sample Spiritual Program:

Here is a spiritual program that is guaranteed to keep your relationship to Christ strong. Again, it is tailored toward Catholics, but, where appropriate, I've suggested some modifications that will be acceptable to Protestant Christians.

Daily Program
Morning
- Morning Offering upon awakening. Raise your mind to God, thank Him for the new day, and ask for his assistance.
- 15 minutes of Mental Prayer.
- Prayer of thanksgiving before breakfast.

Noon
- Pray the Angelus. Protestant Christians may say a short prayer.
- 15 minutes of reading the Bible or some other spiritual book.
- Prayer of thanksgiving before lunch.

Evening
- Dinner together as a family. Say a prayer of thanksgiving for the meal.
- Pray the Rosary as a family or simply pray together as a family.

Before bed
- Conduct a brief examination of conscience of what transpired during the day. Thank God for things that went right and ask for forgiveness for anything that you did wrong.

Weekly Program
- Attend Mass or the weekly worship service at your church as a family. Receive Communion if possible.
- Protestant Christians may also wish to attend a weekly Bible study.

- On Sunday, re-read your marriage vows and review your family mission statement together.
- On Friday, deny yourself some legitimate pleasure. Catholics may abstain from meat. Other suggestions are to pass on dessert or to forego that second cup of coffee. By denying yourself, you are making yourself tougher.

Annual Program

- Participate fully in the liturgical seasons of Advent and Christmas by deeper prayer, fasting, and the giving of alms. Consider the use of an Advent wreath to mark the passing of the season.

- Celebrate feast days by either going to Mass or by reading something about the life of the saint. Protestant Christians can limit themselves to celebrating feast days only of saints that appear in the Bible.

- Observe Lent as a penitential season of prayer, fasting, and almsgiving.

- Celebrate Easter not just as a single day but as an entire season emphasizing Christian joy over the resurrection.

11. Spiritual Headship

Spiritual headship is the concept that the husband is, or should be, the spiritual leader of his family. In the past, this was considered obvious. Men were expected to lead. But with the development of feminism and radical egalitarianism, the idea that the husband should be the leader in a relationship began to be considered as sexist.

That is really unfortunate, because masculine leadership is a necessary ingredient to every successful marriage.

Misunderstandings of Spiritual Headship

Before we discuss what spiritual headship is, it will be helpful to understand what it is not.

The Military Commander

Masculine leadership is not equivalent to the authority of a military commander on the field of battle. In a combat situation, soldiers are expected to obey the orders of their superior without question.

The classic movie, *The Sound of Music*, gives a good portrayal of this kind of a husband. The movie is about the Baron von Trapp and his seven children. The Baron is a widower and a military officer. He runs his house like a military unit—efficient but with little tenderness. It is not until he falls in love with his children's governess that he began to relax his strict ways.

The military commander husband is a good provider and he is faithful to his duty. He doesn't cheat on his wife. But, while he is steadfast, he provides no warmth to his wife and children.

I am not sure if the military commander was ever very common, but it is safe to say that most men today are not tempted to being over disciplined. However, husbands always need to be on guard against becoming emotionally distant from their family.

The Sultan

Another misunderstanding of masculine leadership is that of an oriental potentate who expects a submissive woman. In this model, the woman is there for sex, cooking, and raising children. She is infinitely faithful and obedient. She does not have interests of her own. Instead, the wife of the sultan sacrifices herself for her husband and children.

The husband, on the other hand, gets all the benefits with none of the down sides. While he expects his wife to remain faithful, he can engage in affairs with other women. Unlike his wife, he is free to pursue his self-actualization in whatever career he chooses. Rather than sacrificing himself for the family, he can engage in a life of pleasure.

Unlike the military commander type of leadership, the sultan model occurs more frequently. Although it is less prevalent than it was in the past, men who consider themselves "macho" use the sultan leadership model. This "macho" style of leadership is also more prevalent in some nonwestern cultures.

Enlightened Egalitarianism

Young women are taught by feminism that all masculine leadership is inherently bad. Instead, they are led to believe that enlightened egalitarianism is the only proper model. In this model, there is no spiritual leader in a marriage. Instead, the husband and wife are equal in everyway. Both are supposed to work, do house work, and parent children. Decision-making is to be by consensus.

After the arrival of the egalitarian marriage, everything was supposed to be perfect—only it is not. Women are able to work, but they find that they are still responsible for mothering their children and their husbands, no matter how well intentioned they are, cannot fulfill the role of a mother.

The high divorce rate also signals that women are not happy with their new, sensitive husbands. They view their egalitarian husbands as wimpy, boring, and indecisive so they leave their husbands to search for the exciting "bad boy."

Men and women also seem to be unhappy if the wife is the greater provider in the family. I read an essay by a woman who earns significantly more than her husband so she gives him money before they go out to eat so that he can be the one who pays. Men are also unhappy with the arrangement because they feel emasculated.

I've had my own experience using the egalitarian model. Like most men in the West, I was raised to treat my wife as my equal and that all decision-making should be shared. To my chagrin, I learned that it doesn't work.

One small example is determining when and where to take a vacation. Usually in the late winter, I would broach the topic of vacation and my wife would either show no interest or she would nix my vacation ideas. After being rebuffed, I would shelve the conversation until June. At that point, my wife would finally agree, but by then it was too late. All of the vacation rentals would be booked. The ones that were open were atrociously expensive. We ended up never taking a nice vacation.

It wasn't until I started exercising some leadership in this regard that we were again able to successfully plan a vacation.

So the enlightened egalitarian model doesn't work, but does that mean that we have to go back to the military or sultan model of leadership? Fortunately, true masculine leadership does not involve either of those approaches.

Spiritual Headship

Although the phrase "spiritual headship" does not appear in the bible, the concept derives from scripture. In the first letter to the Corinthians, Paul writes:

> But I want you to understand that the head of every man is Christ, the head of a woman is her husband, and the head of Christ is God (1 Cor. 11:13).

So even though it is not explicitly stated, the implication is clear: Jesus is the leader of the Church as the husband is to be the leader of his family. In his letter to the Ephesians, Paul adds:

> Be subject to one another out of reverence for Christ. Wives, be subject to your husbands, as to the Lord. For the husband is the head of the wife as Christ is the head of the church, his body, and is himself its Savior. As the church is subject to Christ, so let wives also be subject in everything to their husbands.
>
> Husbands, love your wives, as Christ loved the church and gave himself up for her, that he might sanctify her, having cleansed her by the washing of water with the word, that he might present the church to himself in splendor, without spot or wrinkle or any such thing, that she might be holy and without blemish. Even so husbands should love their wives as their own bodies.
>
> He who loves his wife loves himself. For no man ever hates his own flesh, but nourishes and cherishes it, as Christ does the church, because we are members of his body. For this reason a man shall leave his father and mother and be joined to his wife, and the two shall become one flesh."
>
> This mystery is a profound one, and I am saying that it refers to Christ and the church; however, let each one of you love his wife as himself, and let the

wife see that she respects her husband (Eph. 5:21-33).

The two biblical passages I just cited are very controversial in our day. Women especially are so conditioned to assert equality in all aspects of their lives that they react physically when the idea is challenged. I've seen women literally recoil in anger when these passages are read. Some pastors are so terrified of the reaction of their flock that they avoid reading them during the liturgy or church service.

It is really a shame that it has gotten to this point because when the meaning behind these passages is explained, I don't think that many people would find it offensive.

Also, while the concept of spiritual headship derives from the bible, that doesn't mean the concept does not apply to non-Christian relationships. The masculine/feminine dynamic is built into our very being. Therefore, even if you are not believers, your marriage will benefit from applying the following information.

Servant Leadership
The key to understanding the above passages is to understand the type of headship that St. Paul is referring to. Paul does not understand headship in terms of any secular model, but rather in terms of the type of leadership exercised by Jesus—servant leadership.

True leaders do not constantly insist upon the prerogatives of leadership. Instead, they express their leadership by serving others. Jesus explains servant leadership in this way:

> And Jesus called them to him and said to them, "You know that those who are considered rulers of the Gentiles lord it over them, and their great ones exercise authority over them. But it shall not be so among you. But whoever would be great among you must be your servant, and whoever would be

first among you must be slave of all. For even the Son of Man came not to be served but to serve, and to give his life as a ransom for many" (Mark 10:42-45).

Sacrificial Love
Husbands and wives are both to have a sacrificial love for each other. That means that they put the good of their spouse over their own good for the sake of Christ.

For women, this is expressed by being subject to their husbands, "as to the Lord."

For men, the bar is even higher. Husbands are to love their wives "as Christ loved the church and gave himself up for her." In other words, a husband must be willing to sacrifice his very life for his wife.

The ideal described by St. Paul in Ephesians is a two-way street. It would be wrong for a man to "lord it over" his wife, but it would be equally wrong for a woman to belittle or nag her husband.

Limitations to Spiritual Leadership
There are a few limitations to a husband's headship. The first limitation is that the wife does not have to obey her husband if what he says conflicts with right reason. The husband cannot ask his wife to do something immoral or something that would be injurious to her or her children.

A second limitation is that the husband cannot treat his wife like a child. She is not a servant, but his companion. Divine love must guide the husband and wife's mutual relations. The husband cannot "take away the liberty which fully belongs to the woman both in view of her dignity as a human person, and in view of her most noble office as wife and mother and companion" (*Casti Connubii*).

The last limitation is the case where a husband is not a Christian or where he has embraced some sort of error or heresy. In this case, the husband loses his authority to lead the religious worship of his family. The wife's attitude must be that of St. Peter who said, *we must obey God rather than men* (Acts 5:29). He still retains his headship in other matters.

An example will illustrate what I mean. Let's take the case of a Christian couple who gets married, but then later in the marriage, the husband converts to Islam. In this situation, the wife is not obliged to follow her husband and convert to Islam. She should still strive to be a faithful, exemplary wife, and she should pray for her husband.

Masculine Leadership in Practice

So much for the theory, how does spiritual headship work in practice? Here are concrete steps that husbands can take to become the leaders that they are meant to be.

Live as a Servant Leader

The first step is to live the servant leadership of Christ in your life. If you fail in this regard, your wife will never accept your authority. You might be able to get her to follow along by "pulling rank," but it will be unsustainable. Eventually, your wife will begin to resent your authority—and once resentment sets in it can spell doom for a marriage.

Surprisingly, the US Army Ranger creed sheds some light on how to do this:

> Never shall I fail my comrades. I will always keep myself mentally alert, physically strong and morally straight and I will shoulder more than my share of the task whatever it may be, one-hundred-percent and then some.

Although this creed was designed for a military Special Forces unit, the principles in this portion of the creed apply to every leadership situation, even the masculine leadership required in marriage.

Shoulder More Than Your Share

As a husband, it is your duty to never fail your wife and children. It means that you are taking more than your share of the load of work.

Taking more than your share of the work does not mean that you and your wife are splitting all the same work. There is always going to be a division of labor. But it does mean that you are working at least as hard as your wife—it is just the price that you must pay for being a leader.

Keep Physically Strong

Observe that the Ranger creed also says that rangers should be mentally alert, physically strong, and morally straight. This is excellent advice for all husbands. What does it mean practically speaking?

Husbands should stay in good shape physically. That means working out and eating right. It is never acceptable to let yourself go. Being in good shape sets an example for your entire family. If a man let's himself get fat and out of shape, he has no basis to insist that his wife also maintain a healthy weight.

One of the ways that I lead my family in fitness is that I work out with my wife. At first, I didn't think that my wife would enjoy lifting weights, but she quickly came to love it. Now, we motivate each other to work out.

Keep Morally Straight

Husbands should be morally upstanding because they are responsible for setting the moral example for their family. A man who surfs for internet porn or has affairs is not going to have any sort of moral authority with his wife or his children. On the contrary, he will elicit disgust.

But being a good example of moral leadership is not just limited to the sexual sphere. The masculine leader will act ethically in all areas of his life, including his business dealings.

It is also up to the husband to lead the family in matters pertaining to worship. I see too many women taking their children to church while dad stays back. Unfortunately, the mother's good efforts are usually wasted.

Even if the father is not overtly trying to undermine his children's faith, by not asserting his spiritual duties, he will damage their belief. When the father fails to attend church services with his family, the message the children learn is that formal practice of their faith is not important. Without formal practice of a faith, it is easy to slip into not believing.

If you want your children to believe, the father will have to live his faith, not just on Sundays, but on every day of the week. Pray with your children. Let them see you praying and reading your bible.

The husband's example will also affect his wife. The woman will naturally follow her husband's lead if he lives a consistent moral and spiritual life.

Keep Mentally Alert

To be true leaders, husbands must be mentally alert. An army ranger must be on guard against enemy attacks, but to lead a family, fathers need to be alert to risks, opportunities, and areas that require your leadership.

Risks are anything that can disrupt your family. Is there a layoff pending at work? That is an indirect risk on your family. Make plans to mitigate the damage. Is your wife spending an inordinate amount of time texting "friends"? It might be time to talk to her about it. You could be heading off a potential affair.

Opportunities are anything that can help further your position and the position of your family. The masculine leader will always be on the look out for ways to advance his career or for new business opportunities. He will also be aware of ways to provide the best education and formation for his children.

Finally, the husband should be alert to any places in his marriage that can benefit from his servant leadership. There is a big difference between your wife having to ask for your help, and proactively noticing that she does. Being alert allows you to see what needs to be done.

Show Direction
Once you are living as a servant leader, you now have authority. This is not the authority that comes from simply having a title, like a president. It is genuine authority because it is a fruit of your integrity.

But having authority through integrity is not enough. The next step in using masculine leadership is by showing direction.

If a woman does not have masculine leadership, she will naturally try to fill the gap. She will emphasize her masculine traits and assume the role that her husband has abdicated. As I mentioned earlier, this arrangement doesn't make anyone happy. The woman will feel cheated because she must fill two roles. The husband will also be unhappy with a more masculine wife. He may perceive her as being a harpy, a nag, or just too manly.

To show direction, the husband has to be confident and certain about his plans. If a man is uncertain about his direction, his wife will sense it and she will react accordingly. You don't even need to say anything. Your wife will be able to sniff out your uncertainty.

In all large areas of life, the husband should have a well thought out plan that he believes in. In terms of finances, career, and child rearing, the husband should have clear ideas and he should be decisive in implementing them. That doesn't mean that the wife does not have input—she should. It only means that the man is ultimately responsible for charting the course that the family will take.

Having a direction also applies in smaller areas of life. Be decisive! Whether it involves picking out a car seat for your new baby or remodeling the kitchen, have an opinion. Even if you delegate planning to your wife, if she asks for your opinion, provide it. Don't just say, "whatever you think honey."

Accountability

Showing direction also means that you don't let your wife or your children do whatever they want with no accountability.

I have a friend who has taken the modern ideas about independence and trust to the extreme. His wife has developed the habit of going out to dinner and drinking with her girlfriends virtually every night of the week. Most of the time, he comes home from work to have dinner alone.

My friend told me that he is concerned with his wife's behavior, but when I suggested that he talk to her about it he waved the suggestion away. He explained that he and his wife strongly believe that each person in the marriage needs to be fully independent. He also feels that trust is one of the most important things in a marriage. To ask his wife to curtail her dinners would be a violation of trust in his eyes.

Of course, my friend's view is silly. As a husband, he has every right to ask his wife stay home on most evenings. Note that I say, "ask" because if the wife would deliberately go against her husband's wishes it would be indicative of a problem.

The flip side is that husbands are also accountable to their wives. If it were the husband who were going to a bar every night, the wife would have every right to ask that her husband spend more of his time at home. As St. Paul writes, "Be subject to one another."

What If Only One Spouse Lives According to the Ephesians 5 Model?

We've been talking about couples living according to the model outlined by St. Paul in the letter to Ephesians. But what if only one spouse is living according to the biblical ideal? What should the other partner do?

If the husband is failing to be a leader

One of the biggest problems that couples face is the situation where the man is failing to live up to his role as a spiritual leader in the family. This is a common issue because today's men have been indoctrinated in the radical egalitarian philosophy that apart from a few different sex organs, men and women are the same.

If anything, men are taught to defer to women in all things for fear of being sexist. By deferring to his wife, a man may think he is actually an ideal husband.

If your husband has bought into the radical egalitarian ideal or if he just tends to abdicate his masculine leadership, how do you go about getting him to assert his leadership?

The happiest situation is if you are reading this book with your husband. If that is the case, you can simply talk about your perception of his leadership skills. By following the steps given in this chapter, he can begin to assert his natural leadership over his family.

If your husband refuses to read this book, you can still try to improve the situation by living out your femininity. Involve him in decision making by asking for his opinion on things. By treating him as a leader even when he is not acting as one, he may be encouraged to take the reins.

Never assume that your husband is abdicating his leadership role on purpose. Most likely, he is just following the egalitarian script—or he is simply unaware that he needs to be more plugged in.

Unless a man receives solid formation from his father, he is going to enter the marriage a bit ignorant of what his role entails. This was my experience—I wasn't aware that I was dropping the ball in certain areas until my wife pointed it out. I never would have figured it out on my own.

For this reason, you should communicate very clearly what you need from your husband. If you need your husband's input on a project, ask him to get involved. But make sure that you do it in a calm and nonjudgmental way. Assuming that your husband is doing his best will enable you to give feedback without it coming across as an attack.

If the wife is failing to recognize her husband's leadership

Sometimes the problem is that the wife refuses to submit to her husband's spiritual headship. How can the husband assert his masculine leadership?

One way is to have a talk with your wife about it, but I don't recommend that approach. That would be "pulling rank," and while you may be justified in doing it, your wife may react negatively, especially if you don't have a track record of being a servant leader of your family.

Rather, follow the steps outlined under the "Masculine Leadership in Practice" section above. You will find that by living as a servant leader, you will gradually gain your wife's respect, and she will naturally submit to your leadership. Don't expect the process to happen overnight. It may take months of consistent behavior before your wife notices the change.

Tying It All Together

The spiritual headship of the husband is the natural order of marriage. Contrary to what moderns think, spiritual headship is more of a burden than a privilege. Far from making women unhappy, following the biblical design for masculine and feminine roles will ensure that both husband and wife are happy.

12. Fighting for Marriage

One of the best ways to strengthen your own marriage is to fight for the institution of marriage as a whole. But when you talk about strengthening the institution of marriage, people immediately think of political action: electing the right politicians and getting the right justices on the Supreme Court.

While enacting laws that encourage marriage is a good thing, it is far from the only thing you can do to revitalize the institution. In fact, apart from keeping your own marriage strong, the very best way to fight for marriage is to strengthen the marriages of those who are closest to you. Here are some ways to do that.

Teach Your Children

It may seem obvious, but the best way of strengthening marriage is to teach your children about what it takes to have a good one. You'd be surprised at how many parents skip this crucial aspect of educating their children.

In my interactions with young single people, I have been appalled at how little guidance they received from their parents on the most important things in life. Modern parents do a good job of equipping their children to achieve success in the job market, but they often fail to equip them to have a successful marriage. They don't teach their children about what kind of person they should or should not date. Parents also don't provide their children with realistic expectations when it comes to marriage.

Parents are the primary educators of their children, and the most important knowledge that they impart is the wisdom on how to live well. Teach your children about the purpose of marriage, the qualities to look for in a spouse, and how to conduct themselves once they are married.

There are two ways to hand this wisdom to our children: our example and explicit verbal instruction.

Model a Strong Marriage

The ideal way to teach our children about marriage is to model a good marriage. Our children are careful observers. They are watching the way we treat our spouse, the way we act when we encounter adversity, and the way we treat outsiders. They know when we are acting in accord with or contrary to our own values. At every moment, we are teaching our children through our actions.

It is a heavy responsibility for us as parents, but take solace in the fact that our children also realize that we are human. We all have weak moments. If your character is strong, you will pass on good values to your children even if you occasionally fail to live up to those values.

Modeling a strong marriage is good, but what if you have gotten a divorce? Does that mean that you are no longer a credible example to your children?

I once attended a conference for Christian fathers. All of the talks were geared toward fathers who were living with their children. After one of the talks, a man stood up and said, "All of this stuff is great, but I made a mistake. My wife and I divorced and she has custody of our kids. Can I still be a good role model?"

Of course, the answer is a resounding 'yes.' You can still be a strong example to your children despite having gotten a divorce.

First, you can be honest with your children about any mistakes you made in your marriage. What did you learn from the experience that you can pass on to them? While doing this, be very careful to not say anything negative about your ex-wife or ex-husband because it is a bad practice to denigrate your child's other parent. It will hurt your child more than it hurts your spouse.

Second, if you are already remarried, you can use your current marriage as a model for your children to emulate. This is what happened in my own case. My mother divorced my father when I was seven years old. That marriage was terrible, but her second marriage has been very strong so she is a good role model in spite of the divorce.

But Don't Just Teach By Example

However, while modeling a good marriage is the most powerful tool, it is not enough in our current culture to hope that your children get the message merely through observation. To fully equip your children to have successful marriages, you will have to teach them using words as well.

It is a good idea to begin having these conversations early— sometime after you have your first discussion about the "birds and the bees." One of my friends actually includes some of these concepts as part of the discussion about sex, which he calls "God's great plan for love and marriage." The earlier you can introduce these ideas the better.

Teach Your Children the Purpose of Dating

Dating is the modern form of courtship, the process where young men and women determine who they will marry. If a young person believes that the primary reason to date is to find his future spouse, he will be saved from dating a lot of inappropriate people.

For example, I recently witnessed a young couple out on a date. The attractive young lady had red hair and fair skin. She was dressed in a skirt that was probably a little too short. Her date was slightly older, but he was dressed in traditional Muslim garb. He had a beard that was dyed red in imitation of the Prophet Mohammed, which indicated that he was a very devout Muslim. The contrast between the two of them was glaring.

I don't think even the most open-minded, liberal person would admit that this date was a good idea. Being a devout Muslim, the young man would never marry the girl without her converting to his faith. In fact, it was impossible that they could even openly have a boyfriend/girlfriend relationship, as the man's community would frown upon it. While it is easy to see how the young man stood to gain, it is more difficult to see how this relationship could end happily for the girl.

Thus, the first thing that we should teach our children is that they should view dating primarily as a way of finding a future spouse. This will help our children from getting bogged down in dead-end relationships.

That doesn't mean that our children should never date until they are absolutely ready for marriage. There is something valuable about meeting different people of the opposite sex—it helps a person decide what he or she is looking for in a spouse. But there is still no reason to date people who are not even in the ballpark.

Having fun is also a part of dating. But there are other ways to have fun without the overhead involved with a date. Teach your children about the benefits of dating alternatives such as meeting people in group settings. Going out in a group lets young people get to know members of the opposite sex in a fun atmosphere without the intense intimacy that often accompanies a date.

Encourage Married Couples and Single People

Another way to strengthen marriage is to encourage married couples that you know. This doesn't have to be anything formal. The most natural way of doing this is through friendship.

As always, your example is more effective than anything you say. You would be surprised how much you influence people just by being a person who is openly in a committed, happy marriage. People likely look to you as a role model even if you are not aware of it. Your example is the strongest witness to the institution of marriage. In most situations, it is not necessary to "preach" marriage. Your life is testimony enough.

In fact, preaching can sometimes backfire if one's life is not consistent with the principles one espouses. I know a lawyer who is very vocal about his support of marriage, but he frequently flirts with paralegals and women at court. I doubt that his preaching has much positive effect. It might even cause people to think that supporters of marriage are hypocrites.

While living consistently is the best thing you can do to support marriage, sometimes speaking out is necessary. For example, if you have a friend who is denigrating his spouse, you may wish to point out some of her good qualities. If your friend appears to be tempted to stray, giving him a reminder of the consequences may be enough to help him to think logically about outcomes.

If you do choose to encourage people using words, be sure that your intention is to genuinely help the person and not to condemn him or to make yourself feel superior.

And don't forget your single friends and acquaintances. While I was single, I really admired my male friends who were in stable marriages. Their example and words of encouragement kept me going at times when I doubted that a happy marriage was still possible.

Encouraging others to get married and stay married is a task that all successfully married couples are called to do. However, there is a more formal way to support marriage, and that is by formally teaching others.

Teach Others Formally

Getting a job typically requires some type of training. On the high end, medical doctors require several years of postgraduate education, but even blue-collar jobs such as plumbers, electricians, and carpenters usually require an apprenticeship or several months of coursework. Getting married, on the other hand, can be done by anybody without attending even a single introductory class.

When we were preparing for marriage in the Catholic Church, the only requirements were that we have a single counseling session with our pastor and that we attend a daylong seminar on marriage. It wasn't nearly enough. The seminar covered some of the Catholic theology of marriage and some morality, but that left little time to discuss the more practical aspects of marriage such as communication and the handling of finances.

It is no better for couples once they are married. There are few practical classes that couples can take to improve their relationships or to learn how to raise children.

You can make a big contribution to marriage by volunteering to teach some of these classes along with your spouse, or by mentoring younger couples. For most people, the best place to do this is through your church. For example, you could offer a bible study for engaged couples or young married couples.

However, the rate of couples that do not have formal religious beliefs is increasing so many couples will never attend a church. These couples can benefit from concrete advice on marriage. To reach these couples, consider offering a short seminar at your local library or YMCA.

Become a Leader

There are other times when it might be necessary to speak out or even assume a leadership position. For too long, advocates of traditional marriage have been willing to stay on the sidelines and let others make decisions regarding marriage and family with hardly any debate.

If a politician or a political party is advocating policies that would undermine marriage, consider writing an editorial to argue why the policies are detrimental. If you have the resources, you may even consider running for local political office. In order for our political process to work, all sides of an issue should be explored and freely debated. Don't be cowed into silence by political correctness.

Re-create the Village

The final thing that you can do to help your marriage as well as the marriages of others is to build a tribe or village. In the past, a married couple never stood alone. At a minimum, the couple was part of a large extended family consisting of the couple's parents and siblings. This extended family was in turn part of a larger village or tribe. Even though relations between the individual members of the tribe may not have been always friendly, each person in the tribe tended to work for the good of the tribe as a whole.

In the transition from the village to the modern nuclear family, this sense of community has been lost. Never in history have people been so isolated from one another. Each family is an atomic unit that faces a hostile culture alone.

One of the side effects of this atomization is that it makes it harder for an individual family to live in a traditional fashion. If the wife decides to quit her job to raise her children, she may be by herself most of the day with no adult to speak with—all the other mothers in the neighborhood are typically away at work. It makes being a stay at home mom a potentially lonely proposition.

Thus, it is very important to create our own villages even though they do not exist naturally. We can strengthen our marriage and the marriages of others by building our own tribes in the modern world.

There has been a lot of discussion within Catholic circles about how this can be done. There are two broad responses: the Benedict Option and the Escriva Option.

The Benedict Option is a term coined by Rod Dreher. It is named after St. Benedict of Nursia. Benedict was a Roman nobleman who lived in the 6th century in the aftermath of the fall of the Roman Empire.

Benedict left the chaos that prevailed in Rome for the woods, where he retired to pray. As time went on, he gathered a group of likeminded men around himself and they formed a monastic community. This community was self-sufficient—the monks worked to provide for a minimalistic existence. Benedict's monastery eventually gave rise to medieval monasticism and led to the creation of Christendom—the unity of Europe under the banner of the Christian faith.

In the modern day, the Benedict Option involves families moving away from the perverse culture that surrounds them into small, self-sufficient communities of like-minded individuals. Although Dreher does not recommend complete disengagement with the culture, he feels that it is necessary to retreat so that we can raise our children in a wholesome environment. In essence, the Benedict Option assumes that the culture is so corrupt that it is not possible to live in it without partaking of its corruption.

The advantage of the full Benedict Option is that it effectively re-creates the village of the past. Mothers live close to each other so that they are able to assist each other with their children as well provide fellowship.

The second option is the Escriva Option, which was proposed by Austin Ruse. The Escriva Option is named after St. Josemaria Escriva, a 20th century saint. Unlike St. Benedict, St. Josemaria designed his spirituality for people who were living in the world. He encouraged Christians to lead disciplined lives focused on God wherever they happened to find themselves.

Living the Escriva Option involves forming intentional communities of likeminded people without retreating from the world. Ruse describes how this can work:

> Though we would never use such a phrase, my family and I live in such an "intentional community" in Northern Virginia where a grade school in a Church has brought dozens of mission oriented families together. Many in the grade school go on to the local Catholic high schools—Oakcrest for the girls and The Heights for the boys. Others have come to this area for the vibrant home-school community. Many live a little further out, gathered in Front Royal, Virginia around Christendom College and the various Catholic apostolates headquartered there. (Austin Ruse, *The Escriva Option: An Alternative to St. Benedict*, Crisis Magazine, July 2015).

The big advantage of the Escriva Option is that one does not have to physically relocate. You can continue to work in your regular job and still reap the benefits of having a strong network of people you can trust.

The disadvantage of the Escriva Option is that your "village" will be more dispersed. Rather than living in the same neighborhood as you would in the Benedict Option, your close friends may live across town.

Which option is better? There is no right answer, but I believe that the Benedict Option has limitations for families. After all, it was originally designed for single men living in a community—not groups of married couples. Starting up a new community is also difficult, as it requires the agreement of many couples.

Personally, we've chosen the Escriva Option, at least for now. There may come a time when the culture becomes so corrupt or dangerous that retreat is the only option, but we are still far from that point in the US.

Be sure to choose one option. You don't want your marriage, or the marriage of others, to face society alone. If you are lucky enough to have a large extended family, that may be all the support you need. But if you are like most married couples, you'll need to become part of a community that you can rely on.

Tying It All Together

"Charity begins at home." So runs the old saying, and it is true. What you do with your own family and those who are closest to you will ultimately have a greater impact than any sort of political change that is imposed from the top.

13. What to Look For in a Spouse

The person who you select to marry is probably the most important decision you will ever make. Yet most people receive very little guidance on what qualities to look for in a potential spouse. Is it any wonder that so many people end up choosing the wrong person?

If you are still single, you are in luck. The next two chapters are dedicated to you.

This chapter will give you *things to look for* in a future spouse that will help you to pick the right person. The following chapter will discuss *things that you can do* to improve your chances at attracting a good spouse.

Being armed with this information will greatly increase your chances for a successful marriage.

A Word About Love

Before we begin, I want to dispel a couple myths about love.

The first myth is that our culture attributes magical properties to the emotion of love. Love is supposed to be able to turn a hardcore alcoholic into a model father or a prostitute into the perfect wife and mother.

Do these miracles of love sometimes happen? Yes. But they are very rare and you shouldn't bet on it when you are looking for a potential spouse. If that new guy that you have fallen for is a drug addict with a history of repeat criminal offenses, don't think your love is going to change him into a model husband.

The second myth is that once you "fall out of love" with your husband or wife, you can never get it back. Among the "YOLO" (You Only Live Once) crowd, "falling out of love" is even considered a legitimate reason to get a divorce. This is patent nonsense that stems from a misunderstanding of what real love is.

Real Love

Modern culture views love primarily as an emotion. It is the emotion that can lead us to overlook giant flaws in people before we marry them. Moderns will say that it is the *feeling* of being in love that makes a marriage. Once the feeling is gone, so is the marriage.

This is a gross misunderstanding of real love. The kind of love that is operational in a successful marriage is more of an *action* than it is a feeling.

Perhaps the best way to think of it is in terms of self-love. I love myself. But that doesn't mean that I have warm feelings about myself. In truth, I almost never have warm feelings about myself. I may even be angry with myself, particularly if I did something stupid. But being angry with myself does not mean that I do not love myself.

It's the same with your spouse. There might be times in your marriage when you don't feel any affection toward your spouse—or even times when you do not like your spouse. Real love does not bail in those moments. It is in those very times when feelings fail us that love propels us forward.

How Will I Know?

Before I met my wife, I used to wonder how I would know when the "right one" came along. I asked my parents but they simply told me, "you'll know."

While there is an element of truth to my parents' advice—I actually did know once I met my future wife—it sounds too mysterious to be of much help. Here is the breakdown of how it really works.

You will be attracted to your future spouse. You will not want them to get away, and the longer you date them, the more you will want to be with them. With my previous girlfriends, I had to force myself to call them once the initial ardor wore off. That never happened when I was dating my wife. The longer I dated her, the more time I wanted to spend with her.

The attraction that you feel will not be merely physical, although it will certainly include that, it will be an attraction to the whole person.

This is why as you should not approach dating with a rigorous checklist ("my future husband will be six foot two, have black hair, blue eyes, earn over $200,000 per year, support gay marriage and abortion rights, and exclusively drive BMWs, but nothing less than a 6-series"). Rather, use the following list of qualities to help you filter out the good candidates from the bad. Your heart will do the rest.

Attraction

As I just mentioned, the first thing to look for is a person whom you are attracted to.

And by attraction, I mean sexual attraction. Our natural attractions are part of how we are made. Sexual attraction tells us subtle things about the person that we may not be consciously aware of, so it would be a gigantic mistake to ignore this information.

For example, we are *naturally attracted* to healthy looking people. There is a good reason for this: our sex drive is ultimately designed for reproduction. If our sex drive is healthy, it will lead us toward selecting a mate who is healthy and therefore potentially better suited to being a parent.

Some people may be uncomfortable with attraction having its ultimate roots in reproduction. It is important to remember that attraction may also be communicating other subtle cues to us—

156

we just don't know what they are. For that reason, we ignore sexual attraction at our own peril.

When it comes to selecting a husband or a wife, people make one of two errors: either they put too much emphasis on attraction to the exclusion of everything else, or they put too little emphasis on attraction and too much on other factors.

Too much emphasis on attraction

This happens when a man or woman selects a spouse exclusively on the person's attractiveness while ignoring significant flaws. An extreme example of this is when a woman marries a handsome man who happens to be a violent criminal. Attraction is a necessary ingredient, but not the only ingredient required for a healthy marriage.

Too little emphasis on attraction

This happens when a person selects a spouse who they are not attracted to because they may have other good qualities. This may be a temptation for some Christians, especially Christian men, because we are taught that character is the most important thing. After all, the bible says, "beauty is fleeting."

This is the cause of a lot of bad marriages where people "settle" for a person with good character even though that person is unappealing. While it is true that character is the most important factor for the long haul, sexual attraction is a "must have" for a marriage.

Sexual attraction is naturally the first thing that piques our interest in a person. It is what makes a man walk across the room to start talking to a girl. Attraction is what moves the girl to keep talking to the guy. Sexual attraction is also what adds fun and spice to the marriage to keep it strong in the long term.

But, sexual attraction is only the starting point. Once you have a man or woman that you are attracted to, there are still lots of other things to consider.

Developing Healthy Natural Attraction

Before we leave the topic of attraction, it is necessary to mention that many of us have been conditioned to be attracted to the wrong type of person. Before you select a future spouse, make sure that you are attracted to healthy people.

One place where this may manifest is with men who view pornography or frequent strip clubs. Porn deforms our natural attraction. Men who view porn may be attracted to women with fake breasts. Or they may favor the "slutty" look of the porn actresses.

To correct this, men who are looking for a wife should stop using porn or visiting strip clubs long before they enter the quest to find the right girl.

Women, too, can deform their natural attraction. Like men, it could be through idolizing the wrong thing. Girls who spend inordinate amounts of time idolizing "bad boy" hip hop artists may find themselves married to a sad approximation.

Another way that women can compromise their natural attraction is by using the Pill. The Pill stops a woman from ovulating by tricking her body into thinking it is pregnant. During this time, a woman is nesting so she will be attracted to a softer, provider-type of man. In other words, they are more attracted to more feminine men during this period.

Once a woman goes off the Pill, she may find that the man that she selected is unappealing to her natural chemistry. The fact that so many women are on the Pill in our society may account for the fact that we now see so many "beta males" who exhibit few masculine characteristics. Men may be adapting to what women want.

The "cure" for women is easy. Women who are in the market to find a husband should quit taking the Pill long before they enter the dating market. In that way, they will have all of their natural attraction intact so that they can make the right choice.

Character

Good character is the next necessary ingredient to a successful marriage. That girl might be the hottest cheerleader at your university, but unless she has good character, she will be a lousy choice for a wife. But what exactly is character?

The dictionary definition of character is the "mental and moral qualities of a person." Below are some qualities to look for in a man or woman who is "marriage material."

The best way to use this list is to not get deeply involved with someone who exhibits a character flaw. Once you are in a relationship, it is much harder to extricate yourself, especially if you have fallen in love with the person. *Make it a rule to not date people with serious character flaws.* Period.

By the way, you can apply this list to yourself as well to ensure that you have these qualities. Moral qualities are not written in stone. You can change your character through diligent effort. Having these qualities will not just pay off in a happy marriage, good character is also the foundation for success in all areas: financial well-being, physical health, and a happy family life.

Honesty

If a person lies to you or others, they are likely a bad bet for marriage. One of the problems with lying is that it quickly affects a person's character. This is because it is hard to tell just one lie—the liar almost always has to cook up other lies to cover up the first one. It is easy for it to become a habit.

Lying might also be indicative of other character defects. Perhaps the person is lying because they are covering up some embarrassing, illegal, or immoral activity.

But can someone who has been dishonest change? Of course, but if they have been dishonest to you during the courtship phase of your relationship, this is a gigantic red flag. If the person is not honest with you now, what makes you think they will be honest with you when you are married?

Fidelity

If a person cheats on you while you are dating, dump them immediately. It is during the dating phase of a relationship that people should feel the most attraction to one another. If your boyfriend or girlfriend can't be faithful during this time, they are almost guaranteed to stray later.

Addictions

There are all sorts of addictions: drugs, alcohol, gambling, pornography, and sex addiction. These are all red flags for relationships. It is indicative that the person lacks self-control.

While people can conquer these addictions, it is not an easy process. Lots of marriages end up on the rocks because one spouse was not able to control his addiction problem

The better approach is to avoid people who have addictions. If you have an addiction, do the hard work of cleaning up before you get into a relationship.

Diligence and Career

You want your future spouse to be someone with a good work ethic. One of the keys to achieving success in life is hard work.

For women, you will want to find a man who is going to be able to provide for you and for any children that may result from the marriage. He may be really handsome, but if he shows no drive to get out of his parents' basement, you will probably want to keep on looking.

For men, you don't need your future wife to be a high powered corporate attorney or the future CEO of the next big start up, but you do want someone with a good work ethic, even if you plan for your wife to be a stay at home mom after having your children. Managing a household while raising children is hard work. If your girlfriend thinks that being a mom means sipping Kahlua mudslides all day by the pool, you may wish to consider looking elsewhere.

Willingness to be a Parent

Do you want to have children? If so, approximately how many? Does your future spouse agree with you?

This question can make or break a relationship, but I constantly run into couples that never discuss it before they get married. My wife and I are friends with a woman who has become embittered because she desperately wants children but her husband doesn't. I've watched this woman go from being naturally happy to being miserable in just a couple of years.

While I was still single I dated a girl who was a talented artist. We were starting to get serious so I brought up the question about children. She evaded my question for a while, but finally confessed that she would be willing to have one child as a concession. Her real love was creating art. Although it was difficult, we decided to part ways. Just remember, that it is always easier to end a dating relationship than it is to end a marriage.

The bottom line is that before you get serious in a relationship, you must find out how your boyfriend or girlfriend feels about having kids. If they don't agree with what you want, don't waste your time. Move on.

Promiscuity

This is a sensitive subject, but you probably should stay away from someone who has racked up high numbers of sexual partners.

Why? Well, a high notch count may be indicative of a deeper emotional problem. Men who sleep with a large number of women may be trying to compensate for a lack of confidence. Women who have slept with lots of men may have low self-esteem.

A person who has had sex with lots of other people may also find it hard to stop. I've known several men who were womanizers before they got married. After they got married, they quickly fell back into their old habits—right around the time that their wives gave birth to their first children.

Of course, I do believe in repentance and redemption, but repentance does not get rid of inclinations or deep-seated problems. Tread carefully.

Sexuality

It seems that more and more people are coming out to be some variation of male or female—or they self-identify as being something other than heterosexual. The most prominent example is Olympic champion Bruce Jenner who announced that he was transitioning into a woman. The popular media applauds these announcements. We are told that people who do such things are brave. What is not discussed is the effect it has on their families.

What I am about to say used to be considered noncontroversial, but I now feel it is dangerous to say: If you are a woman, try to choose a man who is attracted exclusively to women. If you are a man, try to choose a woman who is exclusively attracted to men. View any person who has "experimented" with a healthy dose of skepticism.

While I am discussing different flavors of sexuality, I should also raise another recent development brought on by books like *Fifty Shades of Grey* by E.L. James and by the ubiquity of pornography—some people have become so depraved that normal sex is boring to them. If you run across one of these types, it is best to move on. There are healthier fish in the sea.

Compatibility and Practical Concerns

I come from a traditional European family. One of the things that I was taught by my grandmother is that when a man is looking for a wife, he has to look not just at the girl's character, but also at her family. A girl who came from a family with a bad reputation should be avoided. Conversely, it was a favorable indicator if both the girl and her family had a good reputation.

Most of us no longer look at whether the people we date come from "a good family." That certainly seems fairer because sometimes people can rise above bad circumstances. On the other hand, when you marry a person you are in some sense marrying your in-laws as well.

There is also the issue of genetics. As science progresses, we are learning that more is determined by our genes than we are comfortable in admitting. There is truth in the old saying that "an apple does not fall from the tree." Perhaps it would be a good idea to put at least a little bit of weight on the idea of coming from a good family.

Another thing that is frequently overlooked, particularly in the United States, are the standard markers of compatibility. Marriages to people who are similar to us are more likely to be successful. You can still see this at work in many places in Europe where people are likely to live in or near the town where they were born. Their spouses also tend to be selected from the same town. Growing up in the same area means that the couple will share similar upbringings.

Here is a list of compatibility factors to be on the lookout for while searching for your future spouse.

Faith

St. Paul advised Christians to not be "unequally yoked" with unbelievers. It is not preached very often anymore, but for Christians this is a positive command that is risky to ignore.

Having the same religion—and a similar degree of fervor in your faith—is essential. Things that seem little while you are dating, like attending worship services together, will grow in importance over your married life.

Once children come into the picture, the question of how they will be raised may be a thorny one. Today, you may think it is okay if your future children are raised in a different faith—but will you feel the same way when the time comes? The safest route is to only date people who share your faith.

Means & Ability

Not too long ago, one of the foremost concerns of single people was whether the person they were dating would have the means to support a marriage. Girls would not consider dating a man who demonstrated that he was lazy because it would be likely that he would be a lousy provider. Men had similar concerns. Would the girl that they were dating make a good wife and mother?

These concerns now seem to take a back seat to romantic love. This is most evident when girls will marry criminals who are serving time, but it can manifest with men as well. Men have been known to fall for women who are suffering from serious drug problems or mental illness in an attempt to "save" them.

Our culture encourages us to ignore means and ability when it comes to romance. If a girl doesn't want to date a guy because he is unskilled, her "friends" may try to make her feel guilty for rejecting him. They may accuse her of being stuck up or materialistic. In reality, she is merely being realistic.

We need to reclaim this practical view of dating and marriage. Women should avoid dating men who cannot provide for a family, and men should avoid women who would not be fit wives and mothers.

Ethnicity and Culture

When selecting a spouse, take their ethnicity and culture into account. Coming from the same ethnic group and cultural background can be helpful. It gives the couple something distinctive to hold in common with each other. This is especially important in a multicultural society.

The Korean community in the US is a great example of how an ethnic group can assimilate into the wider culture without losing the distinctive aspects of its own culture. Although Koreans sometimes marry outside of their ethnic group, the norm is still to marry within the Korean community. It gives the young couple a huge common patrimony and community support in making their marriage stronger.

By the way, Americans whose families have been in the country for generations frequently feel that they have no shared culture. Ironically, this tendency is more pronounced in the majority white population than it is among blacks, who have developed a fairly strong community.

One of the reasons that this opinion prevails is that the American educational system deliberately accentuates the achievements of other cultures, and minimizes the achievements of Americans.

For example, I once had a conversation with an elementary school teacher who was in charge of coordinating her school's "international day." The purpose of the event was to showcase the food, clothing, and art of the various cultures that the students descended from. This teacher told me that she felt bad because unlike the Indian, African, and Asian parents, she had no culture to hand on to her children. Nothing could be further from the truth! America most definitely has a vibrant, distinctive culture that you should honor and value.

Education and Intelligence

The political scientist Charles Murray has documented in his book, *Coming Apart: The State of White America*, the trend among Ivy League attendees to only marry other graduates of Ivy League universities. Murray fears that this development threatens to create a permanent upper class in the US.

I think the reason that people tend to marry within their own education level is because education is often a good proxy for intelligence. Education level can also serve as a shared foundation of knowledge.

Thus, while it should not be ironclad law, it is a good rule of thumb to date someone with a similar education/intelligence level.

Politics

Some couples find it easy to tolerate political differences. The most famous couple that leaps to mind is the marriage of Democrat political consultant James Carville and his wife the Republican political consultant Mary Matalin.

But I believe that most people prefer if their spouse is on the same political wavelength. Political differences do not need to be a deal breaker, but it is something that a couple should come to terms with prior to getting married.

Spending philosophy

In the chapter on money traps, I discussed some of the problems that can be caused if one of the spouses has a spending problem. The best time to catch these issues is while the couple is still dating.

Closely observe the spending habits of the people you date. Do they have to buy things in order to feel good? Do they buy things to impress their friends? Do they have issues with gambling? Are they carrying a lot of debt? If so, it may signal a possible spending problem.

Parental feedback and feedback from friends

Have you ever had a friend who was in a relationship with a person that you knew was wrong for him or her, but you couldn't say anything for fear of destroying the friendship?

I have a friend who is very bitter because her husband cheated on her and divorced her. Rather than blaming her husband, she directed her anger at her family because she feels that they did not do anything to support her marriage.

I was curious so I asked how her family felt about the relationship before she got married. She told me that her family was united in believing that her future husband was a bad egg. They were adamantly opposed to the marriage. In other words, her family saw something in the man's character that my friend was blind to.

It is frequently like that. Those who know us best can often see things that we deliberately close our eyes to. Take the opinions of those who are closest to you—your family and friends—into account when selecting a mate.

This concept is very biblical. In Proverbs 19:20 we are exhorted to "Listen to advice and accept instruction, that you may gain wisdom in the future."

Tying It All Together

While this chapter seems to have a very long list of things to look for, don't feel overwhelmed. You will find that most good people already have many of these qualities. The difficult part is to find someone who possesses all these qualities and who you are attracted to.

If you are dating someone who is missing some of these qualities, you should be cautious. Don't ever count on being able to change fundamental character traits about a person.

The final thing to keep in mind is that it is better to be single than to be married to the wrong person. Don't cling to the person who seems wrong. Mr. or Mrs. Right may be just around the corner.

14. Attract the Man or Woman of Your Dreams

I've been married for eleven years, but the dating market was already rough even back then. Judging from conversations that I have with single people, the situation is 100 times worse today. Rampant promiscuity, consumerism, feminism, and the loss of faith have made it next to impossible to find a decent person, much less a potential spouse.

That is why single people today need to be more prepared than ever before—the competition for high quality mates has never been greater. The best way of doing this is to understand what men and women want in a spouse, and then work to improve those areas.

Although self-improvement is the best way, it is not the easiest. Some people are tempted to look for short cuts that will help them find a husband or wife without the hard work of becoming the best person they can be.

For example, some men are tempted to just apply the principles of "game" to improve their chances at winning over the right girl. While there is nothing wrong with learning good conversation techniques, relying on them alone is a dangerous strategy if your life does not live up to the expectations that you create.

What follows are qualities that all men and women want. These are some universal things that you would want in a good friend. After that I list some other qualities where men and women want different things.

Be forewarned. We've been so conditioned to accept the modern concept that men and women are completely equal that what I am about to say may sound politically incorrect, or even harsh.

However, it is not meant to offend but to equip you to be a success in the dating market.

Universal Qualities That Everyone Wants in a Spouse

There are some things that are basic to being a solid, trustworthy person. In fact, if you do not possess these qualities, you are not yet "marriage material." Be honest when you read through these. Are there any areas where you need to grow?

Honesty

Lying has no place in the life of anyone who aspires to be a good person. Make truth your constant companion.

Industriousness

Being industrious means that we don't waste time or procrastinate. Instead, be employed in useful activities that improve your own life and the lives of others.

Trustworthiness

Trustworthiness means that we do what we say we are going to do. We don't drop the ball.

Faith

Men and women both want a person who has a center—a set of core beliefs that they do not stray from. This doesn't mean that a person must necessarily be religious, only that the person has a code that he will not compromise.

Physical and Mental Health

One of the reasons that people get married is to have children. Therefore, we are naturally attracted to people who are physically and mentally healthy. Insofar as it is within your control, strive for optimum health in both areas. I say, "optimum health," because perfect health is not always achievable.

Freedom from Addictions

Our society is geared to create addictions. Millions of men and women are enslaved by addictions to pornography, drugs, alcohol, food, and gambling. If you are addiction-free, you will be more likely to attract the right person.

Broadness & Energy

The kiss of death in dating is boredom. No one wants to date, much less marry, a boring person. But how does one go about becoming a more exciting person?

The first step is to be a passionate person. Have interests and hobbies that excite you. While people who date you may not share your interests, they will sense your passion.

Having passion is particularly important for men. Men should have a mission in life even before they get married. Girls are naturally attracted to men who are going places.

A second step is to increase your physical energy. The foundation for having a high level of physical energy is eating a healthy diet and getting plenty of sleep and exercise. I offer a free ebook on my website http://honoranddaring.com that gives additional ways of boosting your physical energy.

The final step is to keep up to date on what is happening in the culture. Try to stay abreast of the latest books, movies, and popular music. Keep up with current events. Having a broad base of knowledge will make you a more interesting conversationalist

Specific Qualities

What Men Want in a Woman

Careers

Different men have different feelings about having their wives work. Some men enjoy having a second income to allow the family to live in a manner that otherwise would not be possible. Other men prefer women who would make good stay at home moms. The one thing I think that most traditional men have in common is that they don't require a woman to be a high-powered executive. In fact, a man may even be resentful if his wife brings home a bigger paycheck than he does.

Feminists complain when men who are in their thirties overlook their female peers who may be very accomplished in their career for less accomplished women in their twenties. But this is just a case of men behaving like men.

Young women need to be aware of this dynamic. If a woman has marriage as her goal, she should consider getting married younger instead of waiting until she is sufficiently advanced in her career.

Physical Attractiveness

Men tend to be more visual than women so they are more moved by a woman's physical attractiveness than they are by other factors.

Generally speaking, men prefer thinner women. By saying this, I do not mean that men prefer emaciated women—only that they prefer women whose weight is within a healthy range. That healthy range may be a little less than what feminists would have you believe.

The best guideline for what men prefer is the Body Mass Index measure, or BMI. The National Institutes of Health has a calculator available here:

http://www.nhlbi.nih.gov/health/educational/lose_wt/BMI/bmicalc.htm

Women who would like to appear attractive to men should have a BMI within the "Normal" range, which translates to a BMI of 18.5 to 24.9.

While men like fit women, that doesn't mean that a woman needs to go overboard with physical fitness to be attractive. There is no need to attain extremely low body fat percentages or to sculpt six-pack abs.

If you are in the market for a husband, keep your weight in the normal range, eat a healthy diet, and workout regularly.

Femininity

The dictionary definition of femininity is "having qualities or appearance traditionally associated with women, especially delicacy and prettiness." One of the things that falls under the umbrella of femininity is maintaining one's appearance.

This is a big sore point for feminists. They object that women are "forced" to dress up and use makeup to appear feminine. A woman, they tell us, should be equally appealing to men whether she is plain and frumpy or whether she is dressed nicely.

While I sympathize with women on this point, the truth is that men prefer women who are put together. The *New York Times* recently carried an opinion piece of a psychiatrist, Dr. David J. Hellerstein, who was treating a female patient he calls Greta. He notes that Greta was an interesting person, but that with "her homely dresses and unstylish hairdo, Greta looked like someone you'd see in a 1950s *Good Housekeeping* magazine."

Greta flourished under Dr. Hellerstein's treatment. Her panic attacks went away, her career improved, and she became more confident. The one area of her life that did not improve was her romantic life. Although she desperately wanted to meet a man for a long-term relationship, none of the men she met seemed to have any "spark" for her.

At last Dr. Hellerstein broached a forbidden topic:

> One day, after a bit of hemming and hawing — I

knew it would be a sensitive topic — I raised the obvious: Had she considered getting a makeover? One of her friends, as Greta herself had told me, had recently seen an "image consultant" who recommended a whole new wardrobe, new hairstyle, different makeup. Could that, I asked, possibly be helpful?

"After all," I added, "men tend to judge ... "

Greta bristled, and I stopped midsentence.
"You know," she said, "I look much better when I go on a date. I put on makeup, I dress up. My friends say I look great!"

That shut me up.

Hellerstein observed that since Greta looked dowdy on Mondays through Fridays, it was unlikely that she made great improvements in her appearance on the weekends. He tried to raise the issue with Greta later, again to no avail.

Dr. Hellerstein's opinion piece was widely criticized. He was raked over the coals for having the audacity to suggest that a woman who wanted to attract a romantic partner could increase her chances if she dressed stylishly and used makeup. But I think Dr. Hellerstein was correct, and that Greta was fortunate to have such an honest therapist.

The bottom line is that young women should be aware that while there is a time and place for being relaxed about appearance, paying more attention to dressing, makeup, and hairstyle will pay off in attracting a potential husband.

Sex

Our egalitarian society teaches us that men and women experience sex in the same way. Both men and women, society says, should experiment and be as promiscuous as they want to be. Sexual experimentation is supposed to be liberating.

Society's message on this point is dead wrong. Men and women are very different when it comes to sex. Men and women also experience sex differently. For a woman, sex is for pleasure but it is also tied to her emotions. Sex can make her feel attractive or loved. For women, sex may be a way of getting into a romantic relationship. The real goal is not the sex itself, but the love and commitment of the relationship.

For men, on the other hand, there is little emotional connection from sex. While men might experience a temporary boost in self-confidence from sleeping with a girl, the real reason they do it is because it feels good. For men, sex does not imply any sort of commitment. In fact, the ideal relationship for many men would be one where the female freely "puts out" without requiring any sort of commitment or emotional connection from the man.

Understanding this basic truth about men can save women from a lot of heartache.

I have a friend whose romantic life sadly illustrates what can happen if women have an unrealistic view of men. My friend is highly educated and financially successful, but she is deeply unhappy about her failure to find a husband. She confessed to me that she was regularly engaging in demeaning sex, often with men that she had just met, and who she would never see again. I asked her why she consented to these things, she told me that the fact that men want to have sex with her makes her feel attractive.

I explained to her that single men usually classify women into one of two categories. Either they consider a girl "marriage material" or she is just someone to have casual sex with. Men assign a high value to a woman's virtue. The girls who are considered marriage material tend to be *less* promiscuous than average.

Men have much lower standards for women than they are willing to have casual sex with. Generally, there is no emotional bond or commitment with these women. At best, they are considered "friends with benefits." Men will treat these women with a minimum degree of respect and virtually no honor. Far from indicating that she was attractive, these random men were just using my friend.

My friend told me that she wanted to get married, so I advised her that her dating strategy was having the opposite effect of what she intended. Instead of submitting herself to degrading sex with strangers, I suggested that a better strategy would be to respect herself. That included stopping the one-night stands, spending more time getting in shape, and dressing less provocatively.

Women who want to attract a good husband should understand that their virtue has a high value and that sex is a gift that should be reserved for a man who deserves it—ideally the man who would be the woman's husband. Women should also be aware that lots of men are more than happy to take advantage of them.

What Women Want in a Man

Career

Women want a good provider so they are naturally going to be attracted to wealthy men. At the extreme, some women will overlook age, physical fitness, intelligence, and even character to find a man who will be able to provide them with a comfortable life. However, while most women will not be willing to compromise to marry a professional athlete or a tycoon, all women want a man who can provide for the family.

So to attract the best mate possible, men must apply themselves at everything that makes them more marketable and improves their potential earning power. Training in the practical workings of business, entrepreneurship, and investing are "must haves" for every young man.

Physical Attractiveness

Women are less visual than men. I'm sure you've seen cases of beautiful women who marry less attractive men. But if you are trying to maximize your chances of finding a good wife, it is still very important to look your best.

The starting point is good physical fitness. Unless you are a bodybuilder or elite athlete, men should target having a Body Mass Index measure, or BMI, that falls within the normal range of 18.5-24.9. The National Institutes of Health has a calculator available here:

http://www.nhlbi.nih.gov/health/educational/lose_wt/BMI/bm icalc.htm

The reason why I exclude bodybuilders and elite athletes from using the BMI measure is that it does not account for men with a large amount of muscle mass. Bodybuilders especially may have a BMI that indicates obesity while in reality their body fat percentage is under 10%.

In addition to having a BMI that measures in the normal range, all men will also want to engage in athletic activities. Women want a man who looks good, but they also want a man who can protect them physically if the need arises. The desire for an athletic man may not even be something they are consciously aware of—it is just something that is part of how we evolved. This explains the popularity that jocks have with high school girls.

For this reason, I strongly recommend that every man lift weights. It is not necessary to become a bodybuilder. Just develop enough muscle so that you do not appear to be "skinny fat."

Finally, men will also want to dress well depending on their role in life. Obviously, the dressing requirements for a Wall Street banker are going to be different from a cowboy living in Oklahoma, but in both cases the clothes should be clean, tailored properly, and fashionable.

Masculinity

Just as men prefer feminine women, women prefer masculine men. But what does it mean to be masculine?

Masculinity, just like femininity, is under attack in our culture. Consequently, we are encouraging our girls to act like boys, and demanding that our boys act like girls. We've lost touch with what it means to be masculine.

To be masculine is to be a leader. It means that you have vision and that you are able to shoulder more than your share of the burden without complaining. It means being able to keep calm under pressure, and having the ability to solve problems.

Being masculine means that you are equally comfortable with being at work, with a group of male friends, or enjoying a quiet dinner with a girlfriend. It means that you live with honor and that you do what needs to be done, even if it involves a heroic sacrifice.

Sex

We live in a sex-laden society where the message to young men and women is to start having sex as early as possible. Men are conditioned to see sleeping with many women as a hallmark of true masculinity.

It's not. It is more likely to be indicative of some underlying feeling of inadequacy. I've noticed that the same men who have high notch counts also try to project an image in other ways, such as having a flashy sports car or by dressing in gaudy designer clothing.

In an age where most young men are promiscuous, a man who has a sense of honor and decency is a rarity. Not every woman will appreciate such a man, but the *right woman* will.

With this in mind, I encourage men to have lofty ideals. Take the high road. I believe you will find it to be the most rewarding one in the end.

That said, men shouldn't go overboard and commit the opposite error and become a "white knight."

White knights believe that all women are deserving of being put on a pedestal, and that a "good man" should be willing to excuse any sort of bad behavior from a woman. The problem with being a white knight is that women will sense it and take advantage of the man.

I think all young men end up "white knighting" at some point. My youngest brother spent a few of his college years doing all sorts of favors for a girl who turned out to have zero romantic interest in him. Fortunately for my brother, the only thing he wasted was some time and some gas money. Extreme white knighting, though, can lead a man to marry a woman who cheats on him or who has mental or substance abuse problems.

Do not put women on a pedestal—even the best female is just another human—not some ethereal creature. Not all women are virtuous. While all women (and men) should be respected as human beings, they don't all automatically deserve to be loved, honored, and cherished.

Put Yourself Into Circulation

While self-improvement is necessary to attract the spouse of your dreams, it will not do you any good if you spend all your time at home playing video games. You have to go out into places where you will be noticed if you are a woman or where you can find women if you are a man.

If you are in the market for a spouse, consider yourself always on duty. You never know where you will meet the right person. You might meet him or her at the grocery store, at a coffee shop, or at church. Since you are always on duty, look the part. You don't always have to wear a tuxedo or a cocktail dress, but dress neatly wherever you go.

Make it mandatory to go to places where you might be likely to meet people who share your same passions. Churches, running clubs, museums, political groups, and the gym are great places to meet new people. If your church or gym does not have a lot of single people in your target age group, switch to one that does.

Pay attention when you go out. Flirtation usually starts when two people engage in eye contact. If you are distracted and fail to notice the people around you, you create a wall that will close off any chance of meeting someone.

For women, make sure you are somewhat approachable when you are out. If you surround yourself with a large group of friends you make it much more difficult for a man to walk up to you to begin a conversation. Putting on headphones at the gym or being absorbed in your iPhone has a similar effect of closing you off from possible suitors.

For men, the most important thing to remember is that it is the man's job to pursue the girl—not the other way around, despite what you might see on TV. Cast away all shyness and adopt an attitude of boldness. If you see an attractive unmarried girl, approach her politely and attempt to strike up a conversation. If the conversation goes well, ask her on a date.

If a man is well-dressed, and if he approaches confidently, few girls will be offended. On the contrary, most girls will be flattered that a man is paying attention to them.

Of course, you may be rejected, but that is part of the courtship process. Even the most handsome actors get rebuffed by women. If you do get rejected, don't dwell on it. Learn from any mistakes that you have made and move on.

Relax & Stay Positive

It took me a long time to finally find my future wife. I dated many girls who were very nice, but who I just didn't want to marry. There were times when I despaired of ever finding someone. I even entertained the possibility that I would spend the rest of my life as a single person.

You may experience the same feelings. Regardless of what is happening, don't let it get you down. There are lots of single men and women, and it is just a matter of time until you find the right person.

In the meantime, it is very important that you don't worry. When people start to worry too much about finding a wife or husband, they can give off the vibe of being desperate. Potential dates can sense if someone is desperate, and no one wants to be around a desperate person. Ironically, focusing too much on getting married can actually hinder you from achieving your goal.

So rather than worrying, relax. Use the time while you are single to work on self-improvement. Engage in activities that you enjoy. Broaden yourself. Travel, read widely, and try new things. If you stay positive, you will be ready when the right person crosses your path.

Tying It All Together

Societal changes have made it more and more difficult to find a good person to marry. By making the changes suggested in this chapter you will be able to attract the best possible spouse.

Further Reading

I hope you've enjoyed reading this book. I'm confident that if you implement the principles it contains, your marriage will be well protected from the influence of our degenerate culture.

While the book is over, the conversation is just beginning. Over at my website HonorAndDaring.com, I write helpful articles on family, politics, spirituality, and fitness. I look forward to seeing you there.

78978592R00103

Made in the USA
Lexington, KY
16 January 2018